Study Guide to Accompany
Child Psychology
Second Canadian Edition
Vasta • Younger • Adler • Miller • Ellis

Alastair J. Younger
University of Ottawa

John Wiley & Sons Canada, Ltd.

Library and Archives Canada Cataloguing in Publication

Child psychology, second Canadian edition. Study guide / by Ross Vasta ... [et al.].

ISBN 978-0-470-15678-0

    1. Child psychology--Study and teaching (Higher). I. Vasta, Ross
BF721.C452 2008 Suppl.   **155.4**   **C2008-902003-0**

Production Credits
Acquisitions Editor: Rodney Burke
Vice President & Publisher: Veronica Visentin
Vice President, Publishing Services: Karen Bryan
Publishing Services Manager: Ian Koo
Marketing Manager: Patty Maher
Developmental Editor, Typesetting & Design: Gail Brown
Media Editor: Elsa Passera
Cover Design: Tegan Wallace
Printing & Binding: Printcrafters

Printed and bound in Canada.
1 2 3 4 5 PC 12 11 10 09 08

John Wiley & Sons Canada, Ltd.
6045 Freemont Blvd.
Mississauga, Ontario L5R 4J3
WILEY Visit our website at: www.wiley.ca

Contents

Preface
How to Use This Study Guide

Congratulations on having purchased the study guide to accompany *Child Psychology: Second Canadian Edition.* The purpose of the study guide is to get you actively involved in learning the material in your textbook. Its goal is to help you better learn, understand, and apply the concepts from the textbook. Proper use of the study guide, therefore, will enhance your learning of the material.

The study guide has been designed to facilitate *active* learning. For many students, studying is a passive process. They attend class, read the material, and so on, but in each of these activities they serve as relatively passive targets to whom material is presented. Even when they study, they remain relatively passive—they re-read the text or passages they have highlighted, copy their notes, and so on. Although these strategies are part of studying, they do not involve actively testing your knowledge of the material. In contrast, active learning demands that you take control of the learning process by continually testing your knowledge. This study guide incorporates a variety of techniques that will enable you to evaluate what you have learned and to "zero in" on areas in which your knowledge and/or understanding fall short. The following paragraphs outline specific suggestions concerning how to use the study guide to your best advantage.

Read and Study the Chapter

The first step in using the study guide is to read the chapter in the text carefully. Only after carefully reading the chapter are you ready to use the study guide to help you actively learn the material and to evaluate your learning. Read through each chapter and highlight the most important parts. Pay particular attention to the key terms that are used and the key concepts that are discussed. Once you have read through the chapter, you may then begin using the study guide to assist you in learning and understanding the material in the chapter.

Work Through the Study Guide

The next step is to work through the study guide. Each chapter of the study guide includes the following tools designed to help you actively learn the material: OUTLINE, SHORT-ANSWER QUESTIONS, KEY TERMS, FILL-IN EXERCISES, APPLICATION, USING WHAT YOU HAVE LEARNED, SAMPLE TEST QUESTIONS, and ANSWERS.

Outline

Each chapter begins with an outline. This will be your starting point. The outline is an overview of the contents of the chapter. After carefully reading the chapter, enter your questions, comments, and notes in the space under each topic in the outline. Write down terms or concepts you don't understand with their page numbers and re-read these areas in the chapter.

Short-Answer Questions

Each chapter contains a list short-answer questions. These are more specific than the topics listed in the outline. You may use these to examine your knowledge of the topics discussed in the chapter. After reading the chapter, work through these questions. Check off those you are confident that you know well. Review the material in the textbook for those about which you are less confident, recording the important points from your reading in the space below each objective.

Key Terms

Each chapter contains a list of key terms from the textbook. The key terms provide another way of assessing your knowledge of the material in the chapter. After carefully reading the chapter and completing the learning objectives, go through the list of key terms and define each one. Note each term that you feel uncertain of; this will indicate an area in the textbook that you need to review. After defining the key terms, you should then check that your definitions are correct. Go through the chapter and find the terms you have defined. Key terms that you are unsure of indicate areas of the text that you need to study further.

Fill-in Exercises

Fill-in exercises are another way to test your knowledge of the material in the chapter. These are a series of fill-in-the-blank sentences directly related to material from the chapter in the text. Go through these exercises, filling in the word or words that complete each sentence. Check your answers with those at the end of each chapter in the study guide. If you have a good understanding of the material, you should have a good idea of what words complete each sentence in the fill-in exercises. If you could not think of the word to complete a particular sentence, or it is not clear to you why the answer given is correct, this indicates a topic in the text that should be re-read. These exercises are more specific than the previous exercises. They are a way to test your knowledge of specific facts in each chapter. They don't cover every possible fact, but sample from all topics in the chapter.

Using What You Have Learned and Application

These two sections consist of exercises that test your understanding of the material in the chapter by having you apply your knowledge. In most cases, you will be asked to apply what you have read in the chapter to a situation that is described to you. You may choose to work with other students on these exercises, or you may complete them alone. If you have a good understanding of the material in the chapter, you should be able to apply it to the situations described in these sections.

Sample Test Questions

Once you are confident that you have mastered the material in the chapter, you are then ready to try the sample test questions. These questions give you the chance to try out a practice multiple-choice test of the information in each chapter. As with any exam, read each question and answer thoroughly before attempting to choose the most correct answer. After completing the sample test questions, check your answers against those provided at the end of the chapter in the study guide.

If you answer a question incorrectly, it is important to ask the question "Why?" Sometimes people find that they knew the correct answer but gave an incorrect answer because they didn't read the question carefully, didn't read through all the answers carefully before making their choice, or were just careless and marked the wrong answer. If any of these apply to you, then you have learned something about yourself that will be important to keep in mind when you take a real test—read the question carefully, read all the answers carefully, and check that you mark your choice carefully. On the other hand, if you find that you did not know the correct answer, look up the topic in the textbook and review it. Remember, the purpose of the sample test is not just to get the right answer, but to *know* the right answer and to understand why it is correct. To accomplish this, you must attain a thorough understanding of the entire theory, concept, or information that gave you trouble. Make sure that in addition to understanding why a particular response was the *best* answer, you also understand why the other responses were *not*. This will help you gain a deeper understanding of both the main points and the subtleties of the material in the chapter. This is also a good tactic to apply when taking real multiple choice exams. Not only should you look for the best answer, but you should try to be sure that any other answers are *not* the best.

Answers

Finally, you will find the correct answers for the Fill-in Exercises, the Sample Test Questions, and also for most of the Application and Using What You Have Learned exercises. Check your answers against these, and go back and review those portions of the chapter where your answers were incorrect or where you did not know how to answer.

It would be a mistake to think that using the study guide could in any way *replace* reading the textbook. If this was your intention, I strongly advise you to reconsider. Simply looking at a couple of chapters in the study guide will show you that it was not designed to replace the textbook; it was designed to work hand-in-hand with the textbook to facilitate learning. Proper use of the study guide involves carefully reading each chapter in the textbook. In addition, to do well in your course, you must attend all classes and take good notes. In many classes, professors cover topics that may not be included in the text, or may elaborate on material that is in the text. Thus, even the most careful reading of the text cannot replace attending all classes and taking careful notes.

These are my suggestions for how to use your study guide to its best advantage. Good luck in your course! Most of all, ENJOY LEARNING ABOUT CHILD PSYCHOLOGY!

Chapter 1
Background and Theories

OUTLINE

Use this outline as you read the chapter. Enter your questions, comments, and notes in the space provided. Write down terms or statements you don't understand, with their page numbers.

DEVELOPMENTAL PSYCHOLOGY AND ITS ROOTS

Learning Objective 1.1: Understand the philosophical and historical roots of child psychology.

What is Developmental Psychology?

Why Study Children?

Early Theorists

Pioneers of Child Psychology

ISSUES IN DEVELOPMENTAL PSYCHOLOGY

Learning Objective 1.2: How can we understand the influences of nature and nurture, stability and change, and uniformity and variation on child development?

Nature versus Nurture

Continuity versus Discontinuity

Normative versus Idiographic Development

THEORIES OF DEVELOPMENT: COGNITIVE-DEVELOPMENTAL MODELS

Learning Objective 1.3: Describe two major theories of cognitive development.

Piaget's Theory

Information-Processing Models

THEORIES OF DEVELOPMENT: THE SOCIOCULTURAL APPROACH

Learning Objective 1.4: Describe the sociocultural approach to development.

Vygotsky's Theory

Bronfenbrenner's Ecological Model

THEORIES OF DEVELOPMENT: ENVIRONMENTAL/LEARNING APPROACHES

Learning Objective 1.5: Describe how environmental/learning approaches explain development.

Defining Learning

B. F. Skinner

Types of Learning

Research Classic
Little Albert and Little Peter

Social-Learning Theory

Canadian Contributions
Albert Bandura

THEORIES OF DEVELOPMENT: EVOLUTIONARY AND BIOLOGICAL APPROACHES
Learning Objective 1.6: Understand evolutionary and biological approaches to development.

Behaviour and Evolution

Classical Ethology

Applications to Human Development

SHORT-ANSWER QUESTIONS

Upon completion of Chapter 1, you should be able to discuss the following topics. Check off those you are confident that you can discuss well. Re-read the material in the text for the topics about which you are less confident. Record the important points from your reading in the space below each topic.

1. Outline five reasons why developmental psychologists have concentrated their research on humans during the childhood years.

2. Discuss the major theoretical assumptions of John Locke, Jean-Jacques Rousseau, Johann Gottried von Herder, and Charles Darwin.

3. Explain how John Locke viewed the mind of the newborn and how Rousseau held a contrasting view.

4. Describe the importance of language in Herder's view of development.

5.   Define the principle of *recapitulation,* which developed from Darwin's theory.

6.   Describe the contributions made to developmental psychology by G. Stanley Hall.

7.   Describe the contributions of James Mark Baldwin to the field of child psychology.

8.   Describe John B. Watson's view of how learning takes place.

9.   Discuss Arnold Gesell's views on the relative contributions of heredity and environment to development.

10.   Describe the five stages of development outlined in Freud's psychosexual model.

11.   Explain how Erikson's model of development differs from that of Freud.

12.   Define and explain the following issues in developmental psychology:

Nature versus Nurture

Continuity versus Discontinuity

Normative versus Idiographic Research

13.   Explain how Piaget conceptualized intelligence.

14.   Compare the processes of assimilation and accommodation and describe how they work together, according to Piaget's theory.

15.   Contrast children's thinking during the sensorimotor, preoperational, concrete operations, and formal operations periods.

16.   Explain how information-processing theorists conceptualize cognition as a three-part system.

17.   Compare Vygotsky's sociocultural theory of cognitive development with Piaget's position, focusing particularly on the role of the environment.

18.   Explain why Vygotsky's model of development has been termed a sociocultural approach.

19.   Specify the conditions needed in order to infer that learning has taken place.

20.   How can habituation and dishabituation be considered forms of learning?

21.   Distinguish between respondent and operant conditioning.

22.   Explain how behaviours are learned and unlearned according to the *classical conditioning* approach.

23.   Distinguish between positive and negative reinforcement, and explain how these differ from punishment.

24.   Specify the four processes that Bandura believes underlie observational learning.

25.   Explain how the person, behaviour, and environment interact in Bandura's social-cognitive account of learning.

26.   Specify the four qualities that characterize virtually all innate behaviours, according to ethologists.

27.   Explain what ethologists mean by the term *sensitive period*, using the phenomenon of imprinting as an example.

28.   Explain the basic notions of Bowlby's work and of sociobiology.

29.   Describe two major themes of evolutionary developmental psychology.

KEY TERMS

Upon completion of Chapter 1, you should be able to define the following terms.

Developmental psychology   _____

_____

Tabula rasa   _____

_____

Cultural relativism   _____

_____

Nativism   _____

_____

Natural selection   _____

_____

Recapitulation   _____

_____

Baby biography _____

_____

Zeitgeist   _____

_____

Behaviourism   _____

_____

Maturation   _____

_____

Norms _____

_____

Repression _____

_____

Identification _____

_____

Interactionist perspective _____

_____

Identity _____

_____

Nature versus nurture debate _____

_____

Continuity versus discontinuity debate _____

_____

Normative versus idiographic development _____

_____

Universals of development _____

_____

Genetic epistemology _____

_____

Clinical method _____

_____

Schemes _____

_____

Organization _____

_____

Adaptation _____

_____

Assimilation _____

_____

Accommodation _____

_____

Constructivism _____

_____

Periods _____

_____

Sensorimotor _____

_____

Preoperational _____

_____

Concrete operations _____

_____

Formal operations _____

_____

Tools of intellectual adaptation _____

_____

Dialectical process _____

_____

Internalization _____

_____

Ecological perspective _____

_____

Transactional influence _____

_____

Microsystem _____

_____

Mesosystem _____

_____

Exosystem _____

_____

Macrosystem _____

_____

Chronosystem _____

_____

Learning _____

_____

Reflex _____

_____

Respondent behaviour _____

_____

Operant behaviour _____

_____

Habituation _____

_____

Dishabituation _____

_____

Classical (respondent) conditioning _____

_____

Unconditioned stimulus (UCS) _____

_____

Unconditioned response (UCR) _____

_____

Conditioned stimulus (CS) _____

_____

Stimulus generalization _____

_____

Extinction _____

_____

Operant learning _____

_____

Positive reinforcer _____

_____

Negative reinforcer _____

_____

Punisher _____

_____

Social-learning theory _____

_____

Observational learning _____

_____

Vicarious reinforcement _____

_____

Vicarious punishment _____

_____

Imitation _____

_____

Response inhibition _____

_____

Reciprocal determinism _____

_____

Ethology _____

_____

Modal action pattern _____

_____

Innate releasing mechanism _____

_____

Imprinting _____

_____

Sensitive period _____

_____

Sociobiology _____

_____

Evolutionary developmental psychology _____

_____

FILL-IN EXERCISES

Fill in the word or words that best fit in the spaces below.

1. According to John Locke, the mind of the newborn is like a _____ _____.

2. The emphasis on inborn processes rather than environmental factors as the driving force in human development is referred to as _____.

3. The notion that development of the individual parallels the development of the species is referred to as the principle of _____.

4. The term _____, which literally means "the spirit of the times," refers to a theoretical idea that is generally shared by the scientists of a given period.

5. Gesell established statistical _____, or developmental timetables, describing the usual order in which children display various early behaviours and the age range within which each behaviour usually appears.

6. According to Freud, each child is born with a certain amount of sexual energy called _____, that is biologically guided to certain locations of the body called the _____ _____.

7. "Emergent abilities versus acquired skills" is another label for the issue of _____ versus _____.

8. The issue of _____ versus _____ has two components—one concerns the pattern of development; the other concerns the connectedness of development.

9. _____ research is concerned with identifying commonalities in human development, whereas _____ research is concerned with differences in development from one child to the next.

10. Piaget described his own area of interest as _____ _____, or the study of the nature of knowledge in children.

11. A loosely structured interview format employed by Piaget, in which he asked whatever questions or pursued whatever issues he felt would reveal the child's way of reasoning, is referred to as the _____ _____.

12.   Piaget described intelligence not as something a child *has*, but something a child _____.

13.   A _____ consists of a set of skilled, flexible action patterns through which the child understands the world.

14.   Changing existing cognitive structures to fit with new experiences is called _____.

15.   Attempting to fit a new experience into existing knowledge is called _____.

16.   During the _____ period, the child begins to use symbols, such as words and numbers, to represent the world cognitively.

17.   During the period of _____ operations, children are able to perform mental operations on the pieces of knowledge they possess.

18.   Information-processing theorists view children's cognition as a system composed of _____ parts, which many feel is similar to the operation of a _____.

19.   Vygotsky believed that cognitive development results from a _____ process, in which the child learns through shared problem-solving experiences with someone else, usually a parent or teacher.

20.   Vygotsky used the term _____ to refer to the child's incorporation, largely through language, of bodies of knowledge and tools of thought from the culture.

21.   In Bronfenbrenner's ecological perspective, the system nearest the child, which includes the family, the school, the playground, and so forth is referred to as the _____. Social settings that can affect the child, but in which the child does not participate directly, are referred to as the _____.

22.   Mr. Smith's class has just been shown how to multiply fractions. In order to establish that a pupil has learned this skill, a relatively _____ change in _____ must be demonstrated.

23.   _____ behaviours are controlled by their effects while _____ behaviours are controlled by the stimuli that elicit them.

24.   A young child is accidentally hit by a baseball. He develops a fear of baseball bats, caps, and gloves. This phenomenon is called _____ _____.

25.   As a consequence for her good behaviour, Maria's parents let her watch TV for an extra ½ hour before bed. This consequence is referred to as _____ _____. Jorge, on the other hand, has had his TV time cut as a consequence for not doing his chores. This consequence is referred to as _____.

26.   Children are more likely to imitate a model they have observed if they see that the model has been _____.

27.   Bandura's model of *reciprocal determinism* depicts three influences which affect each other: characteristics of the _____, the _____, and the person's _____.

28.   Bowlby maintained that if _____ and _____ do not form a close emotional bond during the child's infancy (which is therefore a _____ period), the child may have difficulty forming close interpersonal relationships later on.

USING WHAT YOU HAVE LEARNED

A number of important figures in the history of developmental psychology were discussed in this chapter. Match the following historical individuals with the concept with which each is most closely associated.

Concepts	**Figures**
1. Tabula rasa	John Locke
2. Behaviourism	Jean-Jacques Rousseau
3. Repression	Johann Gottfried von Herder
4. Norms	Charles Darwin
5. Identity	John B. Watson
6. Cultural relativism	Arnold Gesell
7. Natural Selection	Sigmund Freud
8. Nativism	Erik Erikson

APPLICATION

Which theory or approach can be seen as the source of each of the following bits of advice given to new parents?

1.   "Children learn the most from what you show them."

2.   "Children must be taught to distinguish right from wrong. Parents must react very differently when their children behave properly and improperly."

3.   "It doesn't matter how much you tell them. The important thing is how much they take in, remember, and use."

4.   "In being a parent, it is important to do what comes naturally."

5.   "Children cannot understand ideas which are too far over their heads."

6.   "Children influence parents at least as much as parents influence children."

7.   "Children don't learn very much all by themselves."

SAMPLE TEST QUESTIONS

1.   The notion of *tabula rasa* can be found in whose view of development?

    a.   John Locke
    b.   Johann Gottfried von Herder
    c.   Jean-Jacques Rousseau
    d.   Charles Darwin

2.   Rousseau viewed children as:

    a.   born with a drive for identity
    b.   a blank slate at birth
    c.   born with a certain amount of sexual energy
    d.   born with an innate sense of justice and fairness

3.   The belief that the subject of psychology should be the study of observable behaviour was held by:

    a.   Gesell
    b.   Watson
    c.   Piaget
    d.   Hall

4.   Watson emphasized _____ in studying development.

    a.   psychosexual stages of development
    b.   how children's thinking changes across age
    c.   objective, observable subject matter
    d.   the development of the typical child

5.   Arnold Gesell's work was primarily focused on:

    a.   stages of cognitive development in children
    b.   stages of psychosexual development
    c.   understanding human development in terms of conditioning
    d.   the development of the typical child

6.   Freud's theory of development would be best described as:

    a.   continuous
    b.   discontinuous
    c.   nativistic
    d.   environmental

7.   Which of Erikson's stages of development corresponds to Freud's anal stage?

    a.   initiative versus guilt
    b.   autonomy versus shame and doubt
    c.   trust versus mistrust
    d.   industry versus inferiority

8.   Most current developmental psychologists can be described as _____, in terms of their views on the nature-nurture issue.

    a.   idiographologists
    b.   environmentalists
    c.   interactionists
    d.   nativists

9.   Investigations of individual differences in children's development are characteristic of:

    a.   idiographic research
    b.   normative research
    c.   continuity research
    d.   discontinuity research

10.   In Piaget's theory, schemes are:

    a.   functions that shape children's behaviour
    b.   sequences of stimulus-response associations
    c.   cognitive structures that reflect underlying knowledge
    d.   strings of commands similar to a computer program

11.   Accommodation is the tendency to:

    a.   use existing knowledge in order to understand new information
    b.   modify existing schemes when confronted with new information
    c.   reconcile biological and environmental influences
    d.   change one's behaviour after a negative reinforcer

12.   The period of formal operations, unlike previous stages, features:

      a.   use of symbols such as words, numbers, etc.
      b.   interest in other individuals
      c.   the ability to perform mental operations on bits of knowledge
      d.   higher-level abstract reasoning

13.   Which would be the least interesting to a researcher working from an information-processing perspective?

      a.   encoding
      b.   reinforcement
      c.   retrieval
      d.   storage in long-term memory

14.   Research on children's learning through shared problem-solving experiences with another, such as a teacher or parent, is likely inspired by which theoretical perspective?

      a.   sociocultural
      b.   social learning
      c.   information processing
      d.   sociobiology

15.   Which of the following processes is not a feature of Vygotsky's theory of development?

      a.   classical conditioning of response
      b.   increasing internalization of cultural knowledge
      c.   language as a tool of thought
      d.   shared problem solving

16.   Which of the following is not a condition necessary to meet a psychologist's definition of learning?

      a.   behaviour must change
      b.   learning must result from practice or experience
      c.   learning is relatively permanent
      d.   material learned must be committed to long-term memory

17.   When a student has done an exceptional job on an assignment, Ms. Bigley gives him or her extra Internet time on the computer as a reward and then announces this reward to the whole class, to motivate them. This is an example of:

      a.   a conditioned response
      b.   reciprocal determinism
      c.   dialectical process
      d.   vicarious reinforcement

18.   Mr. Jones wants to teach his class to stay out of fights. He shows them a demonstration videotape in which the main actor refuses to be drawn into a fight even after other children ridicule him. Which process might well occur after the children see the video?

   a.   observational learning
   b.   reciprocal determinism
   c.   dishabituation
   d.   dialectical process

19.   Imprinting was first extensively studied by:

   a.   Bowlby
   b.   Bandura
   c.   Lorenz
   d.   Bronfenbrenner

20.   Bowlby's theory mixes ethology with:

   a.   social learning theory
   b.   information-processing theory
   c.   Freudian theory
   d.   Piagetian theory

ANSWERS

FILL-IN EXERCISES

1. tabula rasa 2. nativism 3. recapitulation 4. zeitgeist 5. norms 6. libido; erogenous zones
7. nature; nurture 8. continuity; discontinuity 9. normative; idiographic 10. genetic epistemology
11. clinical method 12. does 13. scheme 14. accommodation 15. assimilation 16. preoperational
17. concrete 18. three; computer 19. dialectical 20. internalization 21. microsystem; exosystem
22. permanent; behaviour 23. operant; respondent 24. stimulus generalization
25. positive reinforcement; punishment 26. reinforced 27. person; environment; behaviour
28. mother, child (or infant); sensitive

USING WHAT YOU HAVE LEARNED

1. Locke 2. Watson 3. Freud 4. Gesell 5. Erikson 6. Von Herder 7. Darwin 8. Rousseau

APPLICATION

1. social-learning theory 2. operant conditioning 3. information processing 4. human ethology
5. cognitive-developmental theory 6. ecological systems theory 7. sociocultural approach (Vygotsky)

SAMPLE TEST QUESTIONS

1. a	11. b
2. d	12. d
3. b	13. b
4. c	14. a
5. d	15. a
6. b	16. d
7. b	17. d
8. c	18. a
9. a	19. c
10. c	20. c

Chapter 2
Research Methods

OUTLINE

Use this outline as you read the chapter. Enter your questions, comments, and notes in the space provided. Write down terms or statements you don't understand, with their page numbers.

SCIENTIFIC RESEARCH
Learning Objective 2.1: Understand how researchers use the scientific method to study child development.

The Role of Theory

Objectivity and Measurement

TYPES OF RESEARCH
Learning Objective 2.2: Compare and contrast the research methods commonly used to study children.

Descriptive Research

Correlational Research

Experimental Research

STUDYING DEVELOPMENT
Learning Objective 2.3: Analyze the strengths and limitations of the four basic methods for studying child development as a process.

Longitudinal Research

Focus on Research
The Concordia Risk Study: A Canadian Longitudinal Investigation of Aggressive and Withdrawn Children

Cross-Sectional Research

Combining Longitudinal and Cross-Sectional Research

Microgenetic Studies

OTHER RESEARCH TACTICS
Learning Objective 2.4: Understand the uses of cultural research, comparative research, and psychophysiological methods.

Cultural Research

Comparative Research

Psychophysiological Methods

ETHICAL ISSUES
Learning Objective 2.5: Explain the ethical guidelines for human research that developmental researchers must follow.

Potential Risks

Safeguards

SHORT-ANSWER QUESTIONS

Upon completion of Chapter 2, you should be able to discuss the following topics. Check off those you are confident that you can discuss well. Re-read the material in the text for the topics about which you are less confident. Record the important points from your reading in the space below each topic.

1.   Describe the two important roles of theory in research.

2.   Explain why objective methods are valuable in research, and discuss three ways by which investigators ensure objectivity in their research.

3.   Discuss the strengths and limitations of each of the following descriptive methods:

Observational methods

Interview methods

Case studies

4.   Explain how descriptive research, correlational research, and experimental research differ from one another.

5.   Define and give examples of the following: variable, positive correlation, negative correlation, scatter diagram.

6.   Describe how the independent and dependent variables differ from one another.

7.   Define and explain the use of reversal-replication studies.

8.   Discuss the strengths and limitations of quasi-experimental studies.

9.   Explain the difference between longitudinal and cross-sectional research, and discuss the merits and drawbacks of each approach.

10.   Explain what is meant by a cross-sequential design, and discuss why such a design might be used.

11.   Discuss the advantages and disadvantages of the microgenetic method.

12.   Describe two major approaches to studying the role of culture in behaviour or development.

13.   Discuss two reasons for comparative research.

14.   Outline the 14 ethical standards for research with children, subscribed to by members of the Society for Research in Child Development.

KEY TERMS

Upon completion of Chapter 2, you should be able to define the following terms.

Scientific method _____

_____

Theory _____

_____

Law (principle) _____

_____

Hypothesis _____

_____

Objectivity _____

_____

Descriptive research _____

_____

Naturalistic Observation _____

_____

Observer influences _____

_____

Interview method _____

_____

Case study _____

_____

Variable _____

_____

Correlation _____

_____

Positive correlation _____

_____

Negative correlation _____

_____

Correlation coefficient (*r*) _____

_____

Scatter diagram _____

_____

Independent variable _____

_____

Dependent variable _____

_____

Reversal-replication (ABAB) design _____

_____

Quasi-experimental studies _____

_____

Longitudinal design _____

_____

Cross-sectional design _____

_____

Cohort effect   _____

_____

Cross-sequential design _____

_____

Microgenetic method   _____

_____

Cross-cultural studies   _____

_____

Cultural psychology   _____

_____

Ethnographic methods   _____

_____

Comparative research   _____

_____

FILL-IN EXERCISES

Fill in the word or words that best fit in the spaces below.

1.   A set of statements that describes the relationship between behaviour and the factors that influence it is a _____ .

2.   A specific statement that is well supported by research evidence is called a _____ or _____ .

3.   A statement that simply postulates a relationship is called a _____ .

4.   Theories have two important roles in research. The first is to _____ research findings, while the second is to _____ new research.

5.   Three ways in which child psychology stresses objectivity in research are its focus on _____ behaviour, which must be _____ , and which must also be _____ .

6.   Observing children's behaviour in their day-to-day environments and recording what is seen is called _____ observation.

7.   In observational research, investigators try to minimize the effects of _____ _____, that is, knowing that you are being observed.

8.   _____ observations take place in settings where researchers can control important aspects of the environment in which the child is being observed.

9.   The _____ method involves talking with children or others about events, activities, or relationships in their lives.

10.   When two variables change in the same direction, as do weight and height, the relation is described as a _____ correlation.

11.   The correlation coefficient is a number ranging between _____ and _____ that indicates the direction and _____ of a correlation between two variables.

12.   Correlations can be graphically depicted using a _____ _____ .

13.   A researcher systematically changes or manipulates one variable and looks at the effects of the manipulation on a second variable. The variable manipulated is called the _____ variable, while the variable observed is called the _____ variable.

14.   A reversal-replication design is also known as the _____ design.

15.   To study the persistence or stability of behaviours, or the effects of early experiences on later behaviour, researchers employ a _____ design.

16.   A problem known as the cohort effect is sometimes found in _____ research.

17.   A research method that allows researchers to study changes in important developmental processes *as they are occurring* is the _____ method.

18   Cultural psychologists use _____ methods to gather as much information as possible about cultural practices and values.

19   _____ research is conducted with nonhuman species to provide information relevant to human development.

USING WHAT YOU HAVE LEARNED

In Chapter 2 you learned about different types of research methods that are used in developmental psychology. Below you will find the names of various research methods. Identify which of these methods best describes each of the examples of research studies that follow.

Research Methods

Reversal-Replication Design
Cross-Sequential Design
Cross-Sectional Research
Correlational Research
Longitudinal Research
Experimental Research

1. The relation between children's grades at school and the number of hours they typically spend doing homework is examined.

2. To determine whether taking vitamin C reduces the number of colds children get, a group of children are randomly divided into two groups: one group takes vitamin C daily, the other group takes an inert sugar pill. The number of colds they suffer over a 6-month period is measured.

3. An author of children's books is worried that the words she uses in her story will not be understood by children of all ages. She reads the story to three groups of children—one group is 4 years old, one is 5 years old, and one is 6 years old—and compares between groups in terms of how many words the children don't understand.

4. A researcher follows children's development to examine whether participating in an infant swimming class affects their attitudes toward sports when they reach elementary-school age.

5. A parent couple wonders whether eliminating their child's before-bed drink of juice will reduce his bed-wetting. Before beginning, they record how often he wets his bed for one week. Then, they eliminate his bed-time drink for one week. They then re-introduce his bed-time drink for one week. Finally, they eliminate it again for a week. All the while, they keep a record of the number of nights he wets his bed.

6. A researcher wants to determine the long-term effects of early instruction in reading on children's later reading and writing ability. He also wonders at what age such an early reading program might be most effective. He selects three groups of children, aged 3, 4, and 5 years old, and gives training in reading to each group. He then assesses each group's reading and writing ability two years later, and again four years later.

APPLICATION

Situation

A researcher is concerned that imitation plays a major role in children's beginning to smoke. She is particularly concerned with the role played by television characters who smoke and who are admired by children. She wants to examine whether children are likely to imitate such television models.

Questions to Answer

1.   If she wants to determine whether exposure to television models actually influences children (i.e., a cause–effect relationship), what type of research procedure should she use?

2.   How could she set up such a study?

3.   Suppose she wanted to know if imitation is more likely to occur in older children than in younger children (say, in 12-year-olds compared to 8-year-olds). What research method would she use?

4.   With reference to the 14 ethical standards listed in Table 2–2, what steps should this researcher take to ensure that her research follows ethical standards for research with children? Do you see any ethical problems with this research?

SAMPLE TEST QUESTIONS

1.   A statement that simply postulates a relationship is a:

     a.   theory
     b.   law
     c.   principle
     d.   hypothesis

2.   Descriptive research:

     a.   is used only when other research designs would be unethical
     b.   involves comparing groups of children of different ages
     c.   involves the combination of both cross-cultural and comparative research
     d.   involves no formal attempt to identify the relationships between variables

3.   The number that indicates the direction and strength of the relation between two variables is referred to as a:

     a.   correlation coefficient
     b.   negative correlation
     c.   positive correlation
     d.   scatter plot

4.   A researcher is interested in the impact of television violence on aggressiveness in children. She records the number of violent shows watched over a 1-week period by a group of fourth-grade children and relates it to observations of the children's aggressiveness in the school playground. This study is **BEST** described as:

    a.   cross-cultural   b.   experimental
    c.   correlational   d.   comparative

5.   A hypothetical study of the effects of television violence on children's aggressiveness reveals a correlation of +.83 between the number of violent shows watched each week and children's level of aggressiveness. Based on these findings, which of the following conclusions *might* be true?

    a.   Viewing violent television leads to aggressive behaviour.
    b.   Parents who do not allow their children to watch violent shows may discourage aggressive behaviour in their children.
    c.   Children who are more aggressive may have more of a "taste" for violent shows than those who are less aggressive.
    d.   All of the above

6.   A major difference between an experiment and a correlational study is that in an experimental study we can determine that a _____ relation exists between two variables, whereas in a correlational study we cannot.

    a.   positive
    b.   causal
    c.   strong
    d.   direct

7.   Assume an investigator has found a negative correlation between the amount of vitamin C people take and the number of colds they get. The investigator could safely conclude from this finding that:

    a.   the amount of vitamin C taken and number of colds suffered are related to each other
    b.   people who are immune to colds are somehow compelled to take vitamin C
    c.   taking vitamin C causes people to be more immune to colds
    d.   none of the above

8.   A researcher is interested in the effects of watching *Mr. Rogers' Neighbourhood* on prosocial behaviour in children. She randomly assigns children to one of three groups; one group is required to watch 2 hours of *Mr. Rogers' Neighbourhood* per week, the second group watches 4 hours, and the third group watches 6 hours. After one month, she observes the children in the playground, carefully recording all instances of prosocial behaviour (e.g., sharing, helping, caring, etc.), and compares the three groups of children. This study is best described as:

    a.   descriptive
    b.   correlational
    c.   experimental
    d.   cross-cultural

9.   What is the *independent* variable in the study described in question 8?

    a.   Mr. Rogers
    b.   the amount of *Mr. Rogers' Neighbourhood* viewed
    c.   the amount of prosocial behaviour displayed by the children
    d.   the children

10.   What is the *dependent* variable in the study described in question 8?

    a.   Mr. Rogers
    b.   the amount of *Mr. Rogers' Neighbourhood* viewed
    c.   the amount of prosocial behaviour displayed by the children
    d.   the children

11.   Conducting a(n) _____ study is the only way to infer cause-effect relationships between variables.

    a.   cross-cultural   b.   comparative
    c.   cross-sequential   d.   experimental

12.   A researcher believes that sexism in men increases as they get older. He administers a scale of sexist attitudes (i.e., the higher the score, the more sexist is the individual) to a group of 20-year-old men and a group of 50-year-old men, and finds that the older group scores significantly higher than the younger group. He concludes that sexism does indeed seem to increase as men get older. What is likely a problem with the investigator's interpretation of his findings?

    a.   He has not considered the role of the cohort effect in his study.
    b.   Subject attrition could have played a major role in these results.
    c.   The older men could have become "test wise" to the scale given to them.
    d.   All of the above are likely problems in this study.

13.   What type of design is the study described in question 12?

    a.   cross-sequential
    b.   cross-sectional
    c.   microgenetic
    d.   comparative

14.   An investigator wishes to determine the effects of a preschool language program on children's reading ability in elementary school. She also wants to determine what age would be best to begin the program (e.g., 3-years or 4-years old). What would be the best design to answer these questions?

    a.   longitudinal design
    b.   cross-sectional design
    c.   cross-sequential design
    d.   ABAB design

15.   The most appropriate design to use to determine whether children who have very few friends will develop psychological problems later in adulthood would be a:

a.   comparative design   b.   cross-sectional design
c.   cross-sequential design   d.   longitudinal design

16.   To determine infant auditory preferences, DeCasper and Fifer presented infants with a recording of their mother's voice and a stranger's voice. They measured differences in the sucking rhythms of the infants (using a special pacifier) when presented with each of the two recordings. What is the *independent* variable in this study?

a.   the auditory preferences of the infants
b.   whether the recording was of mother's or a stranger's voice
c.   the sucking rhythm of the infants
d.   the special pacifier

17.   Which of the following is **NOT** a disadvantage of the longitudinal approach?

a.   time consuming
b.   the findings may be outdated by the time the study is completed
c.   subject attrition
d.   differences between age levels could be due to cohort effects

18.   Cross-cultural research:

a.   allows researchers to investigate the universality of various phenomena in human development
b.   identifies similarities in behaviours between human and non-human species
c.   is frequently influenced by the cohort effect
d.   involves a combination of longitudinal and cross-sectional designs

19.   An investigator wishes to examine the consequences of maternal prenatal use of cocaine on the developing fetus. He considers designing an experiment in which women who are pregnant would be randomly assigned to either of two conditions: in one condition they would be administered cocaine, in the other condition they would not. After examining the ethical standards of the Society for Research in Child Development, he decides not to conduct the experiment. Which ethical principle likely most strongly influenced his decision?

a.   confidentiality   b.   anonymity
c.   reporting results   d.   non-harmful procedures

20.   Studies that examine mother-infant relations in non-human species are examples of:

a.   comparative research
b.   cross-cultural research
c.   life-course research
d.   cross-sequential research

ANSWERS

FILL-IN EXERCISES

1. theory   2. law; principle   3. hypothesis   4. organize; guide   5. observable; measurable; quantifiable
6. naturalistic   7. observer influences   8. structured   9. interview   10. positive   11. +1.00, −1.00; strength
12. scatter diagram   13. independent; dependent   14. ABAB   15. longitudinal   16. cross-sectional
17. microgenetic   18. ethnographic   19 comparative

USING WHAT YOU HAVE LEARNED

1. correlational research   2. experimental research   3. cross-sectional research
4. longitudinal research   5. reversal-replication design   6. cross-sequential design

APPLICATION

1. Experimental research

2. Experiment research would involve actually exposing groups of children to models who do or do not smoke (independent variable) and measuring how many children in each group imitate this behaviour (dependent variable). There are serious ethical concerns with such a design. The study could also be correlational, looking for a relation between smoking in participants and in the shows they typically watch.

3. Cross-sectional design

4. The researcher needs to follow all 14 ethical standards relevant to this research. Although there are a number of serious ethical problems with this study (particularly if the experimental method is employed), Principle 1 is particularly relevant, as smoking has harmful consequences for the child. No researcher should conduct research that would encourage or result in harmful consequences to children.

SAMPLE TEST QUESTIONS

1. d	11. d
2. d	12. a
3. a	13. b
4. c	14. c
5. d	15. d
6. b	16. b
7. a	17. d
8. c	18. a
9. b	19. d
10. c	20. a

Chapter 3
Genetics: The Biological Context of Development

OUTLINE

Use this outline as you read the chapter. Enter your questions, comments, and notes in the space provided. Write down terms or statements you don't understand, with their page numbers.

MECHANISMS OF INHERITANCE
Learning Objective 3.1: Identify and describe the mechanisms and processes by which physical and behavioural characteristics are inherited.

Cell Division

Inside the Chromosome

Mendel's Studies

On the Cutting Edge The Human Genome Project

GENETIC DISORDERS
Learning Objective 3.2: Describe different types of genetic disorders and their impact on child development.

Hereditary Disorders

Structural Defects in the Chromosome

Focus on Research: Fragile X Syndrome

STUDYING THE EFFECTS OF GENES ON BEHAVIOUR

Learning Objective 3.3: Describe the influence that genes have on the development of psychological abilities and traits.

Family Studies

Adoption Studies

Twin Studies

Combined Twin-Study and Adoption-Study Approaches

MODELS OF GENE-ENVIRONMENT INTERACTION

Learning Objective 3.4: How do genes and environment interact to influence the development of behaviour?

Gottesman's Limit-Setting Model

Scarr's Niche-Picking Model

Plomin's Environmental Genetics Model

Bronfenbrenner and Ceci's Bioecological Model

SHORT-ANSWER QUESTIONS

Upon completion of Chapter 3, you should be able to discuss the following topics. Check off those you are confident that you can discuss well. Re-read the material in the text for the topics about which you are less confident. Record the important points from your reading in the space below each topic.

1.   Describe and differentiate between mitosis and meiosis.

2.   Describe the importance of each of the following:

      genes

      chromosomes

      DNA

3.   Explain the following principles from Mendel's theory:

      principle of dominance

      principle of segregation

      principle of independent assortment

4.   Outline four revisions of Mendel's principles.

5.   Describe briefly the following hereditary disorders:

      Huntington's disease

      Tay-Sachs Disease

      Phenylketonuria

      Sickle-Cell Anemia

6.   Outline the commonly-found characteristics of Down syndrome.

7.   Describe four disorders of the sex-chromosomes:

8.   Describe the cause and main characteristics of fragile X syndrome.

9.   Describe how each of the following types of studies have been used to study the influence of genes on observable human traits:

family studies

adoption studies

twin studies

combined twin and adoption studies

10.   Explain how monozygotic twins differ from dizygotic twins.

11.   Explain how heredity and environment interact in Gottesman's limit-setting model.

12.   Explain the following types of gene-environment correlations described by Sandra Scarr:

passive gene-environment correlation

evocative gene-environment correlation

active gene-environment correlation

13.   Discuss how the notion of *nonshared environment* in Plomin's environmental genetics model accounts for differences in the characteristics and behaviour of siblings.

14.   Explain why Bronfenbrenner and Ceci refer to their model as *bioecological*.

KEY TERMS

Upon completion of Chapter 3, you should be able to define the following terms.

Chromosomes _____

_____

Autosomes _____

_____

Sex chromosomes _____

_____

Mitosis _____

_____

Meiosis _____

_____

Crossing over _____

_____

Gene _____

_____

Deoxyribonucleic acid (DNA) _____

_____

Alleles _____

_____

Base pair _____

_____

Developmental disability _____

_____

Phenotype   _____

_____

Genotype   _____

_____

Dominant gene _____

_____

Recessive gene _____

_____

Polygenic inheritance _____

_____

Incomplete dominance _____

_____

Codominance _____

_____

Genetic imprinting _____

_____

Identical (monozygotic) twins _____

_____

Fraternal (dizygotic) twins _____

_____

Developmental pacing _____

_____

Behaviour genetics _____

_____

Reaction range _____

_____

Passive gene-environment correlation _____

_____

Evocative gene-environment correlation _____

_____

Active gene-environment correlation _____

_____

Nonshared environment _____

_____

Proximal processes _____

_____

FILL-IN EXERCISES

Fill in the word or words that best fit in the spaces below.

1. Genetic material is organized into chemical strands called _____.

2. Body cells reproduce by the process called _____; germ cells reproduce by the process called _____.

3. The process by which one member of a pair of chromosomes exchanges genetic material with the other member is called _____ _____.

4.   The double helix describes the structure of the _____ molecule.

5.   Genes that guide the production of proteins are _____ genes. Their activities are controlled by _____ genes.

6.   The characteristic of a trait that is expressed or observable is called the _____, while the arrangement of genes underlying a trait is referred to as the _____.

7.   When neither member of a pair of genes is entirely dominant or entirely recessive, the genes display _____ _____.

8.   _____ disease is an example of a genetic disorder caused by a *dominant* gene.

9.   The genetic disease where the body's ability to breakdown phenylalanine is affected is called _____.

10.   Sickle-cell anemia is caused by a _____ *(dominant/recessive)* gene.

11.   Down syndrome is the result of a structural abnormality in the _____.

12.   Identical twins are also referred to as _____ twins; fraternal twins are referred to as _____ twins.

13.   According to Gottesman's limit-setting model, genes do not determine development precisely. Instead they establish a(n) _____ _____ within which development will occur.

14.   According to Scarr's niche-picking model, a(n) _____ gene-environment correlation refers to the situation in which genes and environment affect development similarly, because genetically-set predispositions of the child elicit comparable experiences from the environment.

15.   Plomin's model uses the term _____ environment to refer to presumed aspects of the environment that children experience differently.

16.   Bronfenbrenner and Ceci use the term _____ _____ to refer to interactions between the child and aspects of the microsystem which have positive effects on psychological functioning and which help to maximize expression of the child's genetic potential.

APPLICATION

Situation

Two students enrolled in a developmental psychology class have just read Chapter 3 in the textbook and are discussing how genes and the environment interact. One argues that heredity pretty much determines how we turn out and the environment plays a very small role. The other believes that it really is the environment that is important, particularly when considering psychological characteristics, and that heredity plays a major role only in determining physical characteristics such as body build, hair colour, and so on.

Questions to Answer

1.   Can we really make statements like "heredity is more important than the environment"?

2.   What do we know about the role of heredity in psychological characteristics like intellectual performance, personality, and mental disorders?

3.   What are some of the ways that genes and the environment interact?

4.   How do psychologists go about researching the interaction between genes and the environment?

USING WHAT YOU HAVE LEARNED

In Chapter 3 you read about the role genes play in various psychological characteristics. Think of a characteristic in yourself—maybe a particular skill or ability (e.g., mechanical ability, musical ability, mathematical ability, etc.) or a personality or temperamental characteristic. Now, take a look at your closest relatives (parents, siblings) and compare how similar they are to you in terms of the characteristic. If they are similar, could genes account for the similarity? What other influences need to be considered?

SAMPLE TEST QUESTIONS

1.   Human body cells contain how many chromosomes?

    a.   23 individual chromosomes
    b.   23 pairs of chromosomes
    c.   46 pairs of chromosomes
    d.   the number depends upon the person's gender

2.   Body cells duplicate by the process of:

    a.   dominance
    b.   crossing over
    c.   meiosis
    d.   mitosis

3.   The gametes produced as a result of meiosis contain:

    a.   23 pairs of identical chromosomes
    b.   46 individual chromosomes
    c.   either 23 pairs or 46 individual chromosomes, depending on the individual's gender
    d.   23 individual chromosomes

4.   Crossing over describes the phenomenon by which:

    a.   genetic material is exchanged between chromosomes
    b.   germ cells duplicate
    c.   body cells duplicate
    d.   certain genetic abnormalities occur

5.   The person considered the father of modern genetics is:

    a.   Gottesman
    b.   Ceci
    c.   Mendel
    d.   Huntington

6.   Phenotype refers to:

    a.   a person's inherited genetic makeup
    b.   the observable expression of one's genetic makeup
    c.   a genetic disorder that results from a problem involving the bodily management of protein
    d.   the amount of genetic material shared with members of one's immediate family

7.   Betty has blue eyes. Her parents both have brown eyes. Based on what we know about genetics, we can conclude that:

     a.   both of Betty's parents must carry a dominant gene for blue eyes
     b.   both of Betty's parents must carry a recessive gene for blue eyes
     c.   one of Betty's parents must carry a dominant gene for blue eyes
     d.   Betty cannot be the biological child of these parents

8.   What do colour blindness and phenylketonuria have in common?

     a.   both are caused by a recessive gene
     b.   both are caused by a dominant gene
     c.   both are examples of incomplete dominance
     d.   neither has a genetic basis

9.   If both parents carry the gene responsible for PKU, what is the likelihood of their child having PKU?

     a.   0
     b.   1 in 10
     c.   1 in 4
     d.   3 in 4

10.   If detected early, a special diet can help with:

     a.   phenylketonuria
     b.   sickle-cell anemia
     c.   Huntington's disease
     d.   Tay-Sachs disease

11.   Which disorder appears to be influenced by the age at which a woman becomes pregnant?

     a.   PKU
     b.   Tay-Sachs disease
     c.   Down Syndrome
     d.   Huntington's disease

12.   Monozygotic twins share what percent of the same genes?

     a.   25%
     b.   50%
     c.   75%
     d.   100%

13.   Which set of twins are no more similar in terms of genetic makeup than are any other siblings who share the same parents?

    a.   monozygotic twins
    b.   dizygotic twins
    c.   identical twins
    d.   trizygotic twins

14.   A major problem with the twin study approach is:

    a.   family environment may be more similar for monozygotic than for dizygotic twins
    b.   it is very hard to find monozygotic twins to study
    c.   it is very hard to find dizygotic twins to study
    d.   monozygotic twins are frequently not of the same sex

15.   In which of the following characteristics do genetics **NOT** play a role?

    a.   intellectual performance
    b.   psychiatric disorders
    c.   personality
    d.   actually, genetics play a role in ALL of the above

16.   The pattern of spurts and plateaus in the rate of an individual's physical and mental development is referred to as:

    a.   proximal processes
    b.   developmental pacing
    c.   niche-picking
    d.   crossing over

17.   Which of the following findings is true of the intellectual and cognitive abilities of children living in adoptive homes?

    a.   Stronger correlations have been found between the scores of adoptive children and their adoptive parents than between the children and their biological parents.
    b.   Stronger correlations have been found between the scores of adoptive children and their adoptive siblings than between the children and their biological siblings.
    c.   Stronger correlations have been found between the scores of adoptive children and their biological parents than between the children and their adoptive parents.
    d.   Stronger correlations have been found between the scores of adoptive children and their adoptive fathers than between the children and their biological mothers.

18.   Studies have shown that children whose mothers have schizophrenia are about _____ times more likely to develop schizophrenia than are children of mothers who do not have schizophrenia.

   a.   5
   b.   8
   c.   10
   d.   30

19.   The notion that genes interact with the environment by setting the upper and lower limits of our development was proposed by:

   a.   Gottesman
   b.   Scarr
   c.   Plomin
   d.   Bronfenbrenner

20.   According to Sandra Scarr, during infancy genes exert their effects on the environment in a(n) _____ way.

   a.   evocative
   b.   active
   c.   non-shared
   d.   passive

ANSWERS

FILL-IN EXERCISES

1. chromosomes   2. mitosis; meiosis   3. crossing over   4. DNA   5. structural; regulator   6. phenotype; genotype   7. incomplete dominance   8. Huntington's   9. phenylketonuria (PKU)   10. recessive   11. chromosomes   12. monozygotic; dizygotic   13. reaction range   14. evocative   15. nonshared   16. proximal processes

APPLICATION

1. No. Heredity and the environment are both important. A more useful question would be *how* do heredity and environment exert their effects.

2. Family studies, adoption studies, and twin studies reveal that heredity plays a role in various intellectual abilities, personality and temperament, and psychiatric and behaviour problems.

3. Four models explain how genes and the environment interact: Gottesman's limit-setting model, Scarr's niche-picking model, Plomin's environmental genetics model, and Bronfenbrenner and Ceci's bioecological model.

4. The most common methods involve family studies, adoption studies, twin studies, and combined twin-study and adoption-study approaches.

SAMPLE TEST QUESTIONS

1. b	11. c
2. d	12. d
3. d	13. b
4. a	14. a
5. c	15. d
6. b	16. b
7. b	17. c
8. a	18. c
9. c	19. a
10. a	20. d

Chapter 4
Prenatal Development

OUTLINE

Use this outline as you read the chapter. Enter your questions, comments, and notes in the space provided. Write down terms or statements you don't understand, with their page numbers.

STAGES OF PRENATAL DEVELOPMENT

Learning Objective 4.1: Trace the changes that occur in the three stages of prenatal development.

Conception

The Period of the Zygote (Conception to Second Week)

The Period of the Embryo (Third to Eighth Week)

The Period of the Fetus (9th to 38th Week)

On the Cutting Edge
Families Created by Alternative Methods of Conception

TERATOLOGY

Learning Objective 4.2: Describe the impact of teratogens on prenatal development.

Historical Ideas

General Principles

Types of Teratogens

Focus on Research
The Ottawa Prenatal Prospective Study: A Canadian Longitudinal Investigation of the Effects of Prenatal Marijuana Exposure

NATURAL CHALLENGES
Learning Objective 4.3: Describe the natural challenges that can affect fetal development.

Nutrition

Maternal Experiences and Stress

Parental Age

PREVENTING, DETECTING, AND TREATING BIRTH DEFECTS
Learning Objective 4.4: Discuss the various methods of preventing, identifying, and treating birth defects prenatally.

Prevention

Screening for Abnormalities

Treatment

Ethical Considerations

SHORT-ANSWER QUESTIONS

Upon completion of Chapter 4 you should be able to discuss the following topics. Check off those you are confident that you can discuss well. Re-read the material in the text for the topics about which you are less confident. Record the important points from your reading in the space below each topic.

1.   Discuss how the zygote is created.

2.   Describe what takes place during the first two weeks after conception.

3.   Differentiate between the endodermal, ectodermal, and mesodermal layers of the embryo.

4.   Describe how oxygen and nutrients are passed from the mother to the fetus.

5.   Describe the external changes that take place during the fetal period.

6.   Describe the growth of internal organs, including the nervous system and sex organs, during the fetal period.

7.   Describe the early signs of behaviour that have been observed in the fetus from the third through seventh months.

8.   Explain why the 23rd to 24th week of fetal age is referred to as the *age of viability*. Why are younger fetuses not able to survive if born prematurely?

9.   Discuss the physical and socioemotional implications of common alternative methods of conception.

10.   Describe the six general principles that explain how teratogens act.

11.   Describe the major abnormalities associated with prenatal use of the drug thalidomide.

12.   Describe how each of the following street drugs can affect the fetus:

heroin

cocaine

marijuana

13.   Describe the major findings of the *Ottawa Prenatal Prospective Study*.

14.   Describe the major abnormalities associated with prenatal use of diethylstilbestrol (DES).

15.   Discuss the prenatal effects of the following drugs:

caffeine

nicotine

alcohol

16.   Discuss how environmental chemicals may have teratogenic effects, using the effects of mercury, lead, and polychlorinated biphenyls (PCBs) to illustrate your points.

17. Describe the teratogenic effects of the following maternal infectious diseases:

rubella

herpes

HIV

syphilis and gonorrhea

18. Describe the effects of maternal malnutrition. Why is it difficult to isolate the effects of malnutrition from other factors?

19. Discuss how phenylketonuria in the mother can harm the fetus, even when the fetus is genetically normal.

20. Discuss the problems in interpreting the relation between prenatal stress in the mother and problems in the baby.

21. Discuss the role of parental age (both of the mother and the father) in prenatal development.

22. Discuss the following methods of screening for fetal abnormalities. What does each method involve, when can it be used during pregnancy, what problems can each reveal, and what risks, if any, does each carry?

ultrasound imaging

amniocentesis

chorionic villus sampling

endoscopic fetoscopy

test-tube screening

23.   Compare three methods for treating birth defects—medical therapy, surgery, and genetic engineering. How do they differ, and which holds the greatest promise?

KEY TERMS

Upon completion of Chapter 4 you should be able to define the following terms.

Conception   _____

_____

Zygote _____

_____

Embryo _____

_____

Amniotic sac   _____

_____

Placenta   _____

_____

Umbilical cord   _____

_____

Fetus   _____

_____

Age of viability   _____

_____

Teratogen   _____

_____

Teratology _____

_____

Fetal alcohol syndrome (FAS) _____

_____

Genetic counselling _____

_____

Ultrasound imaging _____

_____

Amniocentesis _____

_____

Chorionic villus sampling (CVS) _____

_____

FILL-IN EXERCISES

Fill in the word or words that best fit in the spaces below.

1. Prenatal development begins at _____, or fertilization, when a sperm unites with an ovum to form a single cell called a _____.

2. The period of the _____ ends about 2 weeks after fertilization. During this period, the _____ settles into the blood-enriched lining of the uterus, a process referred to as _____ .

3. The third to eighth week of pregnancy is referred to as the period of the _____.

4. In the third week, the inner cell mass differentiates into three layers, from which all body structures will emerge. Internal organs and glands develop from the _____ layer. Parts of the body that maintain contact with the outside world develop from the _____ layer. Muscles, cartilage, bones, sex organs, and heart develop from the _____ layer.

5. The _____ is the organ through which the mother and the embryo exchange materials. It is linked to the embryo via the _____ _____, which houses the blood vessels carrying these materials.

6.   The ninth to 38th week is referred to as the period of the _____.

7.   The age of _____ refers to the age at which the infant has a chance to survive if born prematurely. This age is currently around _____ to _____ weeks of fetal age.

8.   External sexual organs in males become apparent by the end of the _____ month.

9.   Fetal activity begins in the _____ month. By the _____ month, brain connections are sufficient for the fetus to exhibit a sucking reflex when the lips are touched.

10.   The discovery and study of the harmful effects of teratogens through the use of behavioural measures is referred to as _____.

11.   _____ affects the fetus indirectly through reduced maternal blood flow to the uterus, limiting the fetus' supply of nutrients and oxygen. It also passes through the placenta and into the fetus' bloodstream, affecting the fetus' heart rate, blood pressure, and chemical nerve transmitters in the brain.

12.   _____ _____ syndrome refers to a unique set of features, including facial malformations and other physical and mental disabilities in the infant and child, caused by the mother's use of alcohol during pregnancy. Some children exposed prenatally to alcohol demonstrate some, but not all, of these effects. Such children are said to suffer from fetal alcohol_____ _____.

13.   Most herpes 2 infections of infants occur following direct contamination by the mother's infected _____ _____.

14   It appears that the _____ virus can be passed on to the baby directly through the placenta prior to birth and also through breast milk following birth.

15.   The fetus is relatively resistant to infection from the syphilis spirochete until the _____ or _____ month after conception.

16.   Diets lacking in _____ are associated with cretinism, a severe thyroid deficiency that causes physical stunting and mental deficiency.

17.   Achondroplasia is a genetic disorder that is related to the age of the _____.

18.   _____ _____ is a non-invasive procedure for detecting physical defects in the fetus that uses soundlike waves to provide a continuous picture of the fetus and its environment.

19.   _____ is a procedure in which a needle is passed through the mother's abdominal wall into the amniotic sac to gather discarded fetal cells to examine for chromosomal and genetic defects.

APPLICATION

Situation

After finishing school, you are planning to begin a family. You want your children to have the best environment to grow up in, beginning with the prenatal environment. You decide to ask for your doctor's advice about pregnancy.

1. After reading Chapter 4, what sorts of precautions do you expect your doctor to give you?

2. If conception became a problem, what alternative methods of conception might your doctor propose?

3. Suppose you were concerned about a genetic disorder present in some of your relatives. What might your doctor suggest to evaluate the chances that the disorder might appear in your children?

4. Your doctor suspects twins! What screening procedures might be used to check this out?

USING WHAT YOU HAVE LEARNED

Many people hold a lot of misconceptions and inaccurate beliefs about pregnancy and prenatal development. You may have encountered some of these beliefs, sometimes held by otherwise well-informed people. After reading Chapter 4 you should be able to argue against many common misconceptions about prenatal development based on what current research has shown. Listed below are some common misconceptions. Based on what you have read in Chapter 4, argue against each of these misconceptions.

1. "The fetus is protected against any harm by the placenta and the amniotic fluid it is surrounded by."

2. "Nutrition is not a problem for the fetus. It is sort of like a parasite: it takes whatever it needs in terms of nutrition from the mother, regardless of what she eats. Although the mother may be malnourished, the fetus is still able to meet its nutritional needs."

3. "If a mother is frightened while pregnant, or if she has unsatisfied cravings for certain types of food, these may show up in birthmarks of a particular shape or colour in the infant."

4. "It is only 'real' drugs that a mother needs to be concerned with. People use things like alcohol, caffeine, or nicotine all the time—they couldn't hurt the fetus."

5. "Marijuana doesn't have any harmful effects on the mother, and it isn't addictive, so it couldn't hurt the fetus."

6.   "If a mother gets sick during pregnancy, the more severe her symptoms, the more likely the disease will affect the fetus."

7.   "With all these things around that can cause birth defects, it's better to decide not to have children. The chances of having a child with a birth defect are very high, and there's nothing you can do about it."

SAMPLE TEST QUESTIONS

1.   The zygote:

   a.   receives 23 pairs of chromosomes from the mother and 23 pairs of chromosomes from the father
   b.   receives 23 chromosomes from the mother and 23 from the father
   c.   receives 23 chromosomes either from the mother or from the father, depending on the gender of the zygote
   d.   contains only 23 individual chromosomes, which will mix with 23 from another zygote at conception

2.   Implantation is a process that takes about

   a.   one week
   b.   two weeks
   c.   three weeks
   d.   four weeks

3.   The period of the embryo ends:

   a.   when implantation begins
   b.   when implantation is complete
   c.   at the end of the eighth week of prenatal development
   d.   at birth

4.   Most internal organs and glands develop from:

   a.   the ectodermal layer   b.   the mesodermal layer
   c.   the endodermal layer   d.   the ectoplasmic layer

5.   Oxygen and nutrients pass from the mother to the fetus, and waste products pass from the fetus to the mother by way of the:

   a.   placenta
   b.   amniotic fluid
   c.   amniotic sac
   d.   birth canal

6.   The period of the fetus lasts:

   a.   from implantation until the eighth week
   b.   from implantation until birth
   c.   from the ninth week until the 24th week
   d.   from the ninth week until birth

7.   Fetal activity begins:

   a.   in the first month
   b.   in the third month
   c.   in the fifth month
   d.   in the seventh month

8.   Twenty-four weeks of age is known as:

   a.   the age of viability
   b.   the age of implantation
   c.   the end of the period of the embryo
   d.   the end of the period of the fetus

9.   The term *teratogen* describes:

   a.   a procedure for detecting possible birth defects
   b.   a method for dealing with infertility
   c.   the development of the prenatal support system—the amniotic sac, placenta, and umbilical
          cord
   d.   a non-genetic agent that can cause malformation in the fetus or embryo

10.   Which of the following statements about teratogens is **NOT** true?

   a.   A teratogen's effect depends on the genetic makeup of the organism exposed to it.
   b.   The effect of a teratogen on development depends partly on timing.
   c.   Teratogens always gain access to the fetus by passing from the mother's blood to that of
          the fetus via the placenta.
   d.   The likelihood and degree of abnormal development increase with the dosage and degree
          of exposure.

11.   Teratogens are **most** likely to affect organ development:

   a.   during the period of the zygote
   b.   during the period of the embryo
   c.   during the period of the fetus
   d.   just before implantation

12.   During which of the following periods of prenatal development are the effects of rubella most severe?

    a.   the first month post-conception
    b.   the second month post-conception
    c.   the third month post-conception
    d.   the fourth month post-conception

13.   Which of the following statements is true concerning the prenatal effects of nicotine?

    a.   The effects of nicotine and smoke on the fetus have not yet been investigated.
    b.   Smoking during pregnancy produces a unique set of malformations in the fetus known as "fetal nicotine spectrum disorder."
    c.   Smoking has been clearly associated with physical defects, such as limb (arm and leg) defects, particularly during the early stages of pregnancy.
    d.   Smokers, on average, have smaller babies that face an increased risk of infant mortality.

14.   The symptoms of fetal alcohol syndrome include:

    a.   a predisposition toward alcoholism
    b.   increased risk for PKU
    c.   developmental disability and learning disabilities
    d.   increased risk for Down syndrome

15.   The disease that most frequently affects the fetus as it passes through the birth canal is:

    a.   cytomegalovirus
    b.   herpes 2
    c.   HIV
    d.   rubella

16.   The fetus is relatively resistant to _____ until the fourth or fifth month post-conception.

    a.   herpes 2
    b.   syphilis
    c.   HIV
    d.   cytomegalovirus

17.   Which of the following disorders is related to the age of the father?

    a.   herpes 2
    b.   HIV
    c.   rubella
    d.   achondroplasia

18. Which of the following statements is true concerning the effects of prenatal anxiety?

   a. Research reveals that a relation exists between maternal prenatal anxiety and later problems in the offspring.
   b. Although the belief that maternal anxiety could affect the fetus is quite old, current research indicates that this is simply not true.
   c. Although anxiety may have psychological effects on the fetus, it cannot produce physical effects.
   d. Experimental evidence has virtually ruled out the role of genetic factors in the effect of maternal anxiety on the fetus.

19. The procedure in which a small tube is inserted through the cervix and into the placenta to collect a small sample of fetal cells is referred to as:

   a. amniocentesis
   b. ultrasound imaging
   c. chorionic villus sampling
   d. test tube screening

20. Which of the following is **NOT** true about ultrasound imaging?

   a. The sex of the fetus can be determined using this procedure.
   b. This procedure can determine if there is more than one fetus.
   c. Defects of the heart, bladder, and kidneys can be revealed using this approach.
   d. There is an increased risk of miscarriage associated with this approach.

ANSWERS

FILL-IN EXERCISES

1. conception; zygote   2. zygote; zygote; implantation   3. embryo   4. endodermal; ectodermal; mesodermal   5. placenta; umbilical cord   6. fetus   7. viability; 23, 24   8. third   9. third; seventh   10. psychoteratology   11. cocaine   12. fetal alcohol; spectrum disorder   13. birth canal   14. HIV   15. fourth; fifth   16. iodine   17. father   18. ultrasound imaging   19. amniocentesis

APPLICATION

1. Proper nutrition; avoidance of unnecessary medications; avoidance of drugs, alcohol, and tobacco; regular medical appointments to monitor the course of the pregnancy.
2. Some methods include donor insemination and *in vitro* fertilization.
3. Genetic counselling advises prospective parents about genetic disorders and the likelihood of their passing on defective genetic traits to their offspring. Amniocentesis, chorionic villus sampling, and test tube screening are all used to identify genetic defects prenatally.
4. Ultrasound imaging can reveal if there is more than one fetus present.

USING WHAT YOU HAVE LEARNED

1. The placenta and amniotic fluid are not a complete barrier; materials may be slowed by this filter, but will not necessarily be stopped.
2. The quality of the mother's nutrition is probably the most important environmental influence on the fetus.
3. This is false. However, research indicates that maternal anxiety and stress can have negative effects on the fetus.
4. Many commonly-used drugs can indeed have negative effects on the fetus.
5. Marijuana has been found to have subtle, long-term effects on the fetus.
6. Certain relatively mild diseases for the mother can have severe teratogenic effects on the fetus.
7. In fact, the vast majority of infants—greater than 90%—are born healthy and normal.

SAMPLE TEST QUESTIONS

1. b	11. b
2. a	12. a
3. c	13. d
4. c	14. c
5. a	15. b
6. d	16. b
7. b	17. d
8. a	18. a
9. d	19. c
10. c	20. d

Chapter 5
Physical Development: Birth, Motor Skills, and Growth

OUTLINE

Use this outline as you read the chapter. Enter your questions, comments, and notes in the space provided. Write down terms or statements you don't understand, with their page numbers.

BIRTH AND THE PERINATAL PERIOD
Learning Objective 5.1: Discuss the stages of labour, the social and cultural factors that influence childbirth, and the assessment of and factors affecting newborn health.

Labour and Delivery

Cultural Attitudes toward Birth

The Concept of Risk

THE ORGANIZED NEWBORN
Learning Objective 5.2: Describe ways in which the infant's behaviour appears to be organized at birth.

States of Alertness

Application
Sudden Infant Death Syndrome

Rhythms

Reflexes

Congenitally Organized Behaviours

MOTOR DEVELOPMENT

Learning Objective 5.3: Trace the development of motor skills in infancy and childhood.

Principles and Sequences

The Nature and Nurture of Motor-Skills Development

Research Classic

Does Motor Development Depend on Practice or on Maturation?

The Psychological Implications of Motor Development

Motor Development in Childhood

THE HUMAN BRAIN

Learning Objective 5.4: Describe the structure and functions of the brain and trace the development of the brain during childhood.

Structure of the Brain

Development of the Brain

Hemispheric Specialization

Studying the Brain

Focus on Research

Brain Specialization and Plasticity

Studying the Brain

PHYSICAL GROWTH

Learning Objective 5.5: Describe the patterns of growth and maturation in development and the factors that influence them.

Growth in Size

Changes in Body Proportion and Composition

Puberty

Factors that Affect Growth and Maturation

SHORT-ANSWER QUESTIONS

Upon completion of Chapter 5, you should be able to discuss the following topics. Check off those you are confident that you can discuss well. Re-read the material in the text for the topics about which you are less confident. Record the important points from your reading in the space below each topic.

1.   Describe the three stages of labour.

2.   Compare maternal and infant mortality rates in Canada with those in other countries.

3.   Discuss how maternal and family characteristics are related to risk for developmental problems in infants.

4.   Contrast preterm babies with SGA babies. What challenges are faced by these babies?

5.   Describe the following assessment tools: Apgar Exam and Brazelton Neonatal Behavioural Assessment.

6.   Discuss how *prematurity stereotyping* may affect parents' perceptions of their infants.

7.   Describe Wolff's states of infant alertness. Explain how these states provide information about an infant's development.

8.   What is *sudden infant death syndrome*? Discuss several risk factors related to this syndrome.

9.   Explain how the newborn's rhythms may affect sleep patterns.

10.   Differentiate between *reflexes* and *congenitally organized behaviours*, providing examples of each and describing their significance in an infant's development.

11.   Describe each of the following reflexes. Indicate the age at which each disappears:

rooting reflex

palmar reflex

Moro reflex

stepping reflex

12.   Discuss each of the following congenitally organized behaviours:

looking

sucking

crying

13.   Explain the principles of *proximodistal* and *cephalocaudal* development, giving examples of each

14.   Discuss how nature and nurture contribute to motor development, according to the dynamic systems approach.

15.   Describe how Gesell used the co-twin control method to assess the roles of nature and nurture in motor development.

16.   What role does motor development play in infants' understanding of their world?

17.   Explain how information is passed along the neuron, discussing the importance of the dendrites, axon, myelin sheath, synapse, and neurotransmitters.

18.   Briefly describe the three major parts of the human brain.

19.   Describe the three stages of brain development: cell production, cell migration, and cell elaboration.

20.   Explain how the left and right hemispheres of the brain are specialized for different tasks.

21.   Discuss the following three techniques used to study brain functioning: PET, fMRI, and ERPs.

22.   Discuss how growth rates differ between boys and girls.

23.   Discuss how growth rate changes across age in terms of body proportion and composition.

24.   Discuss the physical changes that occur at puberty and how adolescents react to these changes.

25.   Discuss how heredity and nutrition affect growth and maturation.

26.   Describe each of the following eating disorders:

anorexia nervosa

bulimia nervosa

obesity

27.   Describe how abuse and psychological trauma can affect physical growth.

KEY TERMS

Upon completion of Chapter 5, you should be able to define the following terms.

Perinatal period _____

_____

Fetal distress   _____

_____

Cesarean section _____

_____

At risk _____

_____

Anoxia _____

_____

Preterm_____

_____

Small for gestational age (SGA) _____

_____

Apgar exam _____

_____

Brazelton Neonatal Behavioral Assessment Scale _____

_____

Electroencephalograph (EEG) _____

_____

Rapid eye movement (REM) sleep _____

_____

Sudden Infant Death Syndrome (SIDS) _____

_____

Reflex _____

_____

Congenitally organized behaviour _____

_____

Postural development _____

_____

Locomotion _____

_____

Prehension _____

_____

Proximodistal _____

_____

Cephalocaudal _____

_____

Dynamic systems approach _____

_____

Neuron _____

_____

Dendrite _____

_____

Axon _____

_____

Myelin _____

_____

Synapse _____

_____

Neurotransmitter _____

_____

Brain stem _____

_____

Midbrain _____

_____

Cerebrum _____

_____

Cerebral cortex _____

_____

Catch-up growth _____

_____

Skeletal maturity (bone age) _____

_____

Puberty _____

_____

Anorexia nervosa _____

_____

Bulimia nervosa _____

_____

Obesity _____

_____

FILL-IN EXERCISES

Fill in the word or words that best fit in the spaces below.

1.   Labour typically begins around _____ weeks after conception.

2.   By the end of the _____ stage of labour, contractions are very intense and occur every 2–3 minutes.

3.   The procedure in which the baby is surgically removed from the uterus is referred to as _____ _____ .

4.   Around 85% of the risk of severe development problems can be attributed to what happens in the _____ period of development.

5.   _____ birth-weight babies are about 25 times more likely to die in the first month of life than babies born at normal weight.

6.   The infant state of _____ _____ is characterized by regular breathing, with eyes closed and no eye movements, and no activity except for occasional jerky movements.

7.   The infant state of _____ _____ is characterized by eyes open and bright, attention focused on stimuli, and relatively low activity level.

8.   The high frequency of _____ activity during infant sleep may help keep nerve pathways active.

9.   Absence of a baby's reflexive responses to external stimuli may indicate _____ to the central nervous system.

10.   Stroking a newborn's cheek causes it to turn its head toward the side that was stroked, a reflex known as the _____ reflex.

11.   The Moro reflex occurs in response to either a sudden _____ , or a sudden loss of head support.

12.   Sucking can be viewed as a _____ _____ behaviour.

13.   An infant's ability to lift and hold her head before she can walk reflects the principle that development proceeds in a _____ direction.

14.   By _____ months of age, a baby should be able to grasp a small pellet between her thumb and forefinger.

15.   The ability to use the hands as tools for such things as eating, building, and exploring is referred to as _____ .

16.   Thelen has found that as infants try to assemble a new motor behaviour from the abilities currently available to them, they go through the following two steps: _____ and _____ .

17.   The brain contains approximately _____ neurons which each have, on average, _____ connections with other cells.

18.   Most neurons are produced between _____ and _____ weeks following conception.

19.   _____ _____ refers to an eating disorder that involves binging on large quantities of food and then vomiting to purge the excess calories consumed.

20.   Obesity is usually defined as weight that is _____ or more over a standard weight for height.

APPLICATION

Situation

Your friend has just given birth to a preterm infant, Peter, at 34 weeks gestation. She knows that you are studying developmental psychology and calls you with the following concerns:

1.   Ever since she was told that Peter scored below average on the Brazelton scale, your friend has been worried that Peter won't be as smart as his sisters and that he'll do poorly in school. How would you reassure her?

2.   The hospital staff is encouraging your friend to visit and hold Peter but she's afraid of hurting him as he looks so weak. Based on your knowledge from Chapter 5, what would you advise her to do?

3.   Your friend heard somewhere that preterm babies will always lag behind full-term babies developmentally. What does research show about the long-term development of such babies?

4.   Your friend continues to compare her baby to her sister's full-term baby, Susie, who was born one week after Peter. Although Peter is older, your friend notices that Susie is easier to soothe and looks stronger. She is concerned that this means Peter has "failure to thrive" syndrome. What do you think?

USING WHAT YOU HAVE LEARNED

Inaccurate beliefs about newborns and their development are common. Many beliefs are based on a person's experiences and are not supported by empirical evidence. Using your knowledge from this chapter, argue against the misconceptions listed below.

1.   "Infants are born without any abilities. Every one of their movements has to be learned from their parents."

2.   "Good parents should be able to get their newborn infant to sleep through the night without waking. If your infant wakes up, it is because you are spoiling him."

3.   "My baby doesn't love me any more. Last month, when I pressed my finger into her hand, she squeezed it tightly. Now she just ignores it."

4.   "Babies cry all of the time. Their crying doesn't mean anything."

5.   "All babies learn to walk the same way. If your baby doesn't crawl before he walks, he'll never walk properly."

SAMPLE TEST QUESTIONS

1. The method or preparing for childbirth using breathing and muscle exercises is attributable to:

   a. Dr. Virginia Apgar   b. Dr. F. Lamaze
   c. Dr. Barry Brazelton   d. none of the above

2. Fetal distress during the birth process is indicated by:

   a. unusually loud crying by the infant   b. breech birth
   c. unusually high or low fetal heart rate   d. a detached placenta

3. For the low-birth-weight infant, which function is most likely to be problematic?

   a. elimination of waste   b. independence of blood circulation
   c. breathing   d. eating

4. Health care professionals use the Brazelton Neonatal Behavioral Assessment Scale primarily to:

   a. predict future intelligence
   b. obtain a sense of the baby's well-being and risk
   c. determine which infants will need special monitoring during the first days of life
   d. assess the level of fetal distress

5. A factor that determines whether infants at risk can achieve normal development is:

   a. auditory and movement stimulation
   b. reduced parental stress
   c. positive parent-child relationship
   d. all of the above

6. When sleeping, a fetus of 25-weeks gestation engages almost exclusively in:

   a. active sleep   b. REM sleep
   c. passive sleep   d. a & b

7. The purpose of REM sleep in early infancy is to:

   a. regulate respiration   b. exercise the eye muscles
   c. stimulate nerve pathways   d. stimulate growth of brain cells.

8. As the infant gets older, time spent in active sleep:

   a. increases   b. decreases
   c. increases then decreases   d. does not change

9.   Which statement about the sleep-wake cycle of infants is true?

   a.   It is governed primarily by environmental influences.
   b.   Newborn cycles of active and quiet sleep are about the same in duration as adult cycles.
   c.   By 12 to 16 weeks, the pattern of sleeping at night and being awake during the day is fairly well established.
   d.   All of the above are true.

10.   The absence of the Moro reflex at birth:

   a.   indicates disturbance of the central nervous system
   b.   reflects normal neurological development
   c.   occurs with all full-term infants
   d.   indicates that the infant is ready to walk

11.   Congenitally-organized behaviours are unlike reflexes in that they:

   a.   do not occur in response to specific stimuli
   b.   occur in response to specific stimuli
   c.   disappear as the infant develops
   d.   are learned through modelling

12.   Which principle is illustrated by infants' ability to reach for a toy with all fingers extended before they are able to pick it up using their forefinger and thumb?

   a.   proximodistal development
   b.   cephalocaudal development
   c.   prehension
   d.   dynamic systems analysis

13.   One of the functions of the myelin sheath surrounding the axon is to:

   a.   protect adjacent axons from dendrites
   b.   speed axonal message transmission
   c.   provide a reservoir for neurotransmitters
   d.   receive activity from nearby cells and conduct it to the neurons

14.   The part of the brain responsible for balance and coordination is the:

   a.   brain stem   b.   midbrain
   c.   cerebrum   d.   cerebral cortex

15.   _____ continues years after the birth of the infant.

   a.   cell production   b.   cell migration
   c.   cell elaboration   d.   none of the above

16.   Which statement about the development of the primary motor area is false?

   a.   It is the first area of the cerebral cortex to mature.
   b.   Maturation of this area can be indexed by myelin formation.
   c.   Locations that control the head and arms mature before those controlling legs and fingers.
   d.   Development follows in a proximodistal progression, but not in a cephalocaudal manner.

17.   Which of the following statements is false?

   a.   The left side of the brain is more active during language tasks and the right side is more active during mathematical tasks.
   b.   Tasks such as reading and listening involve both sides of the brain.
   c.   Problems with reading performance are sometimes associated with right-brain dominance for language.
   d.   Hemispheric specialization appears late in childhood, just before puberty.

18.   The effect of genetic factors on growth is illustrated by the fact that:

   a.   MZ twins show more similar pace of bone development than do DZ twins
   b.   Asian, European, and African children reach puberty at different ages and move through puberty at different rates
   c.   children with recessive genes achieve smaller stature than children with dominant genes
   d.   a & b

19.   In addition to contributing to slower growth, undernutrition may interfere with:

   a.   intellectual development
   b.   social stimulation
   c.   production of brain cells and myelin
   d.   all of the above

20.   Anorexia nervosa is:

   a.   an eating disorder involving food binging and purging
   b.   an eating disorder involving excessive weight loss through starvation
   c.   an eating disorder defined as weight 20% or more *below* a standard weight for height
   d.   none of the above

ANSWERS

FILL-IN EXERCISES

1. 38   2. first   3. cesarean section   4. prenatal   5. Low   6. deep sleep   7. alert inactivity   8. REM
9. damage   10. rooting   11. sound   12. congenitally organized   13. cephalocaudal   14. nine
15. prehension   16. exploration; selection   17. 100 billion; 3,000   18. 10; 26   19. bulimia nervosa
20. 20%

APPLICATION

1. Although the Brazelton Scale does a fairly good job of characterizing how a baby is doing in the early period, it is not a good predictor of later development.
2. Various forms of gentle stimulation, including rocking and gentle massage, appear to assist the early development of low-birth-weight babies. Handling the infant also increases the mother's confidence in her ability to care for the infant.
3. Development in the preterm baby may lag behind that in a full-term baby, at least for a time. The resources available to the family can also be important. By 2 to 3 years of age, children born preterm into families that have strong financial resources seem indistinguishable from children born at term.
4. It is important to avoid *prematurity stereotyping,* the tendency to expect negative behaviour from premature infants, which can affect how parents interact with the infant.

USING WHAT YOU HAVE LEARNED

1. Newborns possess a number of reflexes and congenitally organized behaviours.
2. Newborn states occur as internally controlled rhythms that gradually adapt to the 24-hr light-dark cycle.
3. The grasping response is a reflex—it increases during the first month and then gradually declines and is gone by three to four months.
4. There seem to be three types of crying in the very young infant: a hungry or basic cry, a mad or angry cry, and a pain cry.
5. Some babies never crawl before walking.

SAMPLE TEST QUESTIONS

1. b   11. a
2. c   12. a
3. c   13. b
4. b   14. a
5. d   15. c
6. a   16. d
7. c   17. d
8. b   18. d
9. c   19. d
10. a   20. b

Chapter 6
Sensory and Perceptual Development

OUTLINE

Use this outline as you read the chapter. Enter your questions, comments, and notes in the space provided. Write down terms or statements you don't understand, with their page numbers.

ISSUES IN THE STUDY OF PERCEPTUAL DEVELOPMENT
Learning Objective 6.1: Explain the issues for understanding perceptual development.

TOUCH AND PAIN, SMELL AND TASTE, MOTION AND BALANCE
Learning Objective 6.2: Outline the development of the basic sensory capacities such as touch, smell, taste, and vestibular sensitivity.

Touch and Pain

Focus on Research
Measuring Pain in Young Children from Facial Behaviour

Smell and Taste

Vestibular Sensitivity

HEARING

Learning Objective 6.3: Describe the development of infants' sensitivity to auditory information.

Prenatal Hearing

Sensitivity to Sound

Discriminating Sounds

Sound Localization

VISION

Learning Objective 6.4: Outline infants' capacity for processing visual information.

Sensory Capabilities

Research Classic
What do Babies See? The Work of Robert Fantz

Visual Pattern and Contrast

Visual Relations

Face Perception

Focus on Research
Face Perception during Early Infancy

On the Cutting Edge
Can Newborns Recognize the Mothers' Faces?

Objects and Their Properties

The Spatial Layout

INTERMODAL PERCEPTION
Learning Objective 6.5: Gain an understanding of how infants integrate the information from different senses that come from a single event.

Exploratory Intermodal Relations

Intermodal Representation

ATTENTION AND ACTION

Learning Objective 6.6: Sketch the development of infants' ability to allocate their attention and to use that attention to guide their behaviour.

Infancy

Older Children

Application
ADHD: Helping Children with Attentional Problems

SHORT-ANSWER QUESTIONS

Upon completion of Chapter 6, you should be able to discuss the following topics. Check off those you are confident that you can discuss well. Re-read the material in the text for the topics about which you are less confident. Record the important points from your reading in the space below each topic.

1.   Distinguish between the processes of sensation, perception, and attention.

2.   Discuss how perceptual development can be viewed as involving both nature and nurture.

3.   Discuss how touch is important for relations between children and adults.

4.   Discuss the likes and dislikes of newborns in terms of smell and taste.

5.   Discuss how investigators have examined the relation between vestibular and visual perception in infants.

6.   Explain how researchers have used the habituation-dishabituation procedure to assess infant abilities to differentiate sounds.

7.   Discuss how researchers have concluded that the fetus can hear.

8.   Discuss the hearing abilities of infants in terms of sensitivity to sound, ability to distinguish differences in intensity and frequency, and ability to localize sound.

9.   Discuss how researchers have assessed visual acuity in newborns and what we know about the visual acuity of infants.

10.   Explain how Robert Fantz examined visual preferences in infants.

11.   Discuss what is known concerning colour vision and pattern perception in infants.

12.   Describe how researchers have examined whether newborns are attracted to human faces. Can newborns recognize their mother's face?

13.   What are the visual constancies? Discuss how researchers have assessed *size constancy* in infants.

14.   Describe what researchers have found concerning *object continuity* in infant perception.

15.   Explain how the visual cliff has been used to assess infant depth perception.

16.   Describe and explain the differences between 2-month-old and 9-month-old infants in their reaction to the visual cliff.

17.   Indicate how crawling may be related to fear of depth.

18.   Explain how infants use pictorial cues and kinetic cues to perceive depth.

19.   Differentiate between *egocentric coding* and *allocentric coding* in the infants' understanding of locations in space.

20.   Describe what Linda Acredolo found concerning how 6-, 11-, and 16-month-old babies use landmarks for keeping track of locations in space.

21.   Explain what is meant by the term *prepared relations*.

22.   Discuss the ability of infants to form haptic-visual and auditory-visual intermodal representations.

23.   Discuss the importance of the following in controlling the infant's attention:

       pop-out

       inhibition of return

       absolute versus *relative* properties of stimulation

24.   List the five rules for acting that govern the looking activity of newborns.

25.   Describe four important aspects of attention that, according to Flavell (1985), develop with age.

26.   Outline the contributions of both nature and nurture to ADHD.

27.   Describe how action skills develop through the school years.

KEY TERMS

Upon completion of Chapter 6, you should be able to define the following terms.

Sensation   _____

_____

Perception   _____

_____

Attention   _____

_____

Haptic perception

_____

_____

Vestibular sensitivity

_____

_____

Preference method

_____

_____

Visual acuity

_____

_____

Visual accommodation

_____

_____

Size constancy

_____

_____

Shape constancy

_____

_____

Brightness constancy

_____

_____

Colour constancy

_____

_____

Visual cliff

_____

_____

Pictorial cues

_____

_____

Kinetic cues _____

_____

Motion parallax _____

_____

Orienting reflex _____

_____

Defensive reflex _____

_____

Selective attention _____

_____

Attention-deficit hyperactivity disorder (ADHD) _____

_____

FILL-IN EXERCISES

Fill in the word or words that best fit in the spaces below.

1.   The detection and discrimination of sensory information is referred to as _____, whereas the interpretation of sensations is referred to as _____.

2.   The soothing properties of rocking and jiggling clearly demonstrate _____ sensitivity in the newborn.

3.   Electrical recordings of brain responses demonstrate sound reception in fetuses as early as the _____ week after conception.

4.   Newborns hear relatively better at _____ (*low/high*) frequencies.

5.   As the size of an infant's head increases with age, the distance between the two ears also increases. This requires an appropriate _____ on the part of the infant in order to localize sounds accurately.

6.   The visual acuity of normal adults is around 20/20. The newborn's visual acuity has been estimated at about _____ to _____. By _____ months of age, the visual acuity of infants approximates that of adults.

7.   In terms of colour vision, newborns can discriminate both _____ and _____ from white.

8.   Looking at a face, young infants tend to look near the _____ of the face, paying relatively little attention to the _____ detail.

9.   As an object moves farther away from us, its image in the eye shrinks. Yet, the object continues to appear the same size. This phenomenon is called _____ _____.

10.   Gibson and Walk assessed infants' perceptions of depth using the _____ _____, a unique device with an apparent drop off.

11.   In perceiving depth, infants can make some use of kinetic depth cues between _____ and _____ months of age. Response to most pictorial static cues is not evident until _____ to _____ months.

12.   Inborn relations between sensory modes—that is, relations for which the baby is predisposed by biology but that are modifiable by experience—are referred to as _____ relations.

13.   After sucking on either a nubby or smooth nipple, 1-month-old infants stared longer at a picture of the nipple they had sucked. This demonstrates intermodal transfer between _____ and _____ perception.

14.   _____ attention refers to concentration on a stimulus or event with accompanying disregard for other stimuli or events.

15.   Finding your white car is easy when the other cars in the parking lot are all black, because of the phenomenon known as _____.

16.   Flavell identified four important aspects of attention that develop with age: _____, _____, _____, and _____.

17.   Approximately _____% of children with ADHD have a relative with ADHD, usually a parent or sibling, suggesting that ADHD may have a biological component.

APPLICATION

Situation

It is common in many cultures for mothers to sing lullabies to their babies. While there seems to be little doubt that mothers enjoy singing to their babies, babies cannot tell us whether they likewise enjoy the lullabies—or can they?

Questions to answer

1. Based on your knowledge of infant auditory perception, is there any evidence that would lead us to believe that babies would enjoy hearing their mothers sing to them?

2. Following examples of research from the text, such as the work of DeCasper and Fifer, how would you design a study to examine whether infants enjoy hearing lullabies sung by their mothers?

3. Suppose you find that babies do enjoy it when their mothers sing to them. How could you test whether it is the music that they like or the fact that it is their mother's voice?

4. In terms of research in auditory-visual relations and facial perception, what sorts of behaviours on the part of the baby might serve to reinforce the mother's singing to the baby (assuming, of course, that the baby is awake)?

USING WHAT YOU HAVE LEARNED

1. William James, the "father" of psychology in North America, described the newborn's reaction to the world as "one great blooming, buzzing confusion." [*] Based on what you have read about infant sensory and perceptual abilities, how would you respond to James' description?

2. The text warns against attributing too much skill to the infant (i.e., the "superbaby" craze). Are there abilities that do seem fairly well-developed at birth? What abilities do you think people might be inclined to overestimate in the young infant?

3. Not long ago, hospitals routinely operated on newborns without anaesthetic, under the assumption that newborns cannot feel pain. Based on what you have read in chapter 6 about the newborn's sensory abilities, what is your opinion about such practices?

---

[*] *James, W. (1890).* The principles of psychology. *New York: Henry Holt, p. 488.*

SAMPLE TEST QUESTIONS

1. The detection and discrimination of sensory information is known as:

   a. sensation
   b. perception
   c. attention
   d. identification

2. Which of the following examples best describes perception?

   a. the ability to distinguish a high tone from a low tone
   b. the recognition of a particular song
   c. not noticing the words of a song because the individual is attending to its tune
   d. identifying the musical instrument that is playing a tune

3. A philosopher named Molyneux described a situation where a man who was born blind is suddenly able to see. Molyneux asked the question whether this man, who had come to recognize objects only by touch when he was blind, would be able to recognize them by sight alone now that he can see. Which of the following approaches would most likely answer "Yes" to Molyneux's question?

   a. the Gibsonian approach
   b. the environmental/learning approach
   c. the empiricist approach
   d. both b and c

4. The earliest that sensitivity to touch can be seen is:

   a. immediately at birth
   b. by the end of the first week after birth
   c. by one month of age
   d. even before birth

5. Infants appear able to recognize the odour of their mother:

   a. immediately after birth
   b. even prior to birth
   c. within the first week of life
   d. this ability emerges slowly across the first four months of life

6. The soothing properties of rocking and jiggling for crying babies demonstrate:

   a. haptic perception
   b. vestibular sensitivity
   c. proximal stimulation
   d. recalibration

7.   Which of the following is **NOT** effective in soothing crying babies?

   a.   speaking to the infant in a high tone
   b.   speaking to the infant in a low tone
   c.   placing a hand on the infant's chest
   d.   gently stroking an infant

8.   Research by DeCasper and colleagues concerning newborns' auditory preferences demonstrated all of the following except:

   a.   newborns showed a preference for their mother's voice
   b.   newborns showed a preference for their father's voice
   c.   newborns showed a preference for a familiar over a novel story
   d.   actually, **all** of the above were found to be true

9.   Newborns of French-speaking mothers can discriminate French from Russian, even when spoken by the same woman. This finding indicates that:

   a.   the fetus is listening to and picking up information about the sounds its mother makes
   b.   the nativist view applies to language; infants have a preference for their "native" language
   c.   French is likely a more basic language than Russian
   d.   certain languages are much easier for newborns to understand than other languages

10.   Compared with normal adult visual acuity of 20/20, the acuity of a newborn is around 20/400 to 20/800. But, by 3 months of age it is:

   a.   20/20
   b.   20/100
   c.   20/200
   d.   20/300

11.   Which of the following is true?

   a.   newborns show a preference for the high contrast borders of a face
   b.   newborns prefer their mother's face over that of a stranger
   c.   newborns are fascinated by the internal features of a face
   d.   newborns prefer colour photographs of faces over black and white photographs

12.   Recent research has found that newborns may recognize their mother's face:

   a.   by attending to the inner details of the face
   b.   by attending to her eyes alone
   c.   by attending to her hairline and the shape of her head
   d.   newborns *cannot* recognize their mother's face

13.   Which of the following does not appear to be present to some degree at birth?

    a.   size constancy
    b.   shape constancy
    c.   colour constancy
    d.   actually, all of the above ARE present at birth

14.   Visual accommodation—the automatic adjustment of the lens of the eye to produce a focused image of an object—is almost adult-like by what age?

    a.   by the end of the first week
    b.   by one month
    c.   by three months
    d.   by six months

15.   Infants as young as _____ notice the difference between the deep and safe sides of the visual cliff, though they may not react with fear.

    a.   one month
    b.   two months
    c.   three months
    d.   four months

16.   When moved from the safe side to the deep side of the visual cliff, the heart rate of _____ increased.

    a.   2-month olds
    b.   5-month olds
    c.   9-month olds
    d.   12-month olds

17.   All of the following help babies to perceive depth, except

    a.   motion parallax
    b.   pictorial cues
    c.   kinetic cues
    d.   recalibration

18.   Flavell identified four important aspects of attention that increase with age. Which of the following is NOT one of those four aspects?

    a.   planfulness
    b.   adjusting
    c.   adaptability
    d.   accommodation

19.   When an experimenter asks children to judge whether two complex pictures are the same, older children systematically compare each detail across pictures, one by one. This aspect of attention is described by Flavell as:

    a.   accommodation
    b.   adaptability
    c.   adjusting
    d.   planfulness

20.   Which of the following is NOT true of ADHD?

    a.   ADHD may be associated with abnormalities in the frontal lobes of the cortex
    b.   ADHD runs in families
    c.   children usually outgrow ADHD by adolescence
    d.   boys are diagnosed with ADHD more often than girls

ANSWERS

FILL-IN EXERCISES

1. sensation; perception   2. vestibular   3. 25th   4. low   5. recalibration   6. 20/400; 20/800; 12 months
7. red; green   8. borders; interior   9. size constancy   10. visual cliff   11. one, three; six, seven
12. prepared   13. haptic; visual   14. selective   15. pop-out   16. control, adaptability, planfulness, adjusting
17. 50

APPLICATION

1.   Newborns show a preference for their mother's voice.
2.   Present a recording of a lullaby and use the infants' sucking rate to measure preference.
3.   Present the mother singing versus simply the melody of the lullaby. Or, present the mother singing
      versus a stranger singing same lullaby.
4.   Infant may orient, look toward mother's face, track movements, etc.

SAMPLE TEST QUESTIONS

1. a	11. a
2. b	12. c
3. a	13. c
4. d	14. d
5. c	15. b
6. b	16. c
7. a	17. d
8. b	18. d
9. a	19. d
10. b	20. c

Chapter 7
Cognitive Development:
The Piagetian Approach

OUTLINE

Use this outline as you read the chapter. Enter your questions, comments, and notes in the space provided. Write down terms or statements you don't understand, with their page numbers.

PIAGET'S THEORY
Learning Objective 7.1: Define the concepts from biology that Piaget used to explain cognitive development and evaluate his theory of stages.

COGNITION DURING INFANCY: THE SENSORIMOTOR PERIOD
Learning Objective: 7.2: Trace the substages and benchmarks of the sensorimotor period in child development.

Studying Infant Intelligence

The Six Substages

Object Permanence

Testing Piaget's Claims: More Recent Work on Infant Cognition

Canadian Contributions
René e Baillargeon

An Overall Evaluation

THOUGHT IN THE PRESCHOOLER: THE PREOPERATIONAL PERIOD

Learning Objective 7.3: Identify some strengths and limitations of preoperational thought in children's cognitive development.

More about Representation

Strengths of Preoperational Thought

Limitations of Preoperational Thought

MIDDLE CHILDHOOD INTELLIGENCE: THE CONCRETE OPERATIONAL PERIOD

Learning Objective 7.4: Analyze the cognitive task masteries that characterize concrete operational thought.

A Sampling of Tasks

The Concept of Operations

More on the Preoperational-Concrete Operational Contrast

ADOLESCENT AND ADULT: THE FORMAL OPERATIONAL PERIOD

Learning Objective 7.5: Explain the characteristics and outcomes of formal operations compared with concrete operations.

Characteristics of Formal Operational Thought

A Research Example: Reasoning about Pendulums

More Recent Work on Formal Operations

EVALUATION OF PIAGET'S THEORY
Learning Objective 7.6: Explain the general characteristics of Piaget's theory and evaluate the theory overall.

Stages

Universality

Cognitive Change

Application
Piaget and Education

NEW DIRECTIONS
Learning Objective 7.7: Discuss and describe more recent research of children's cognitive development that has been influenced by Piaget's cognitive-developmental approach.

Concepts

Theory of Mind

Application
Beliefs about the Causes of Illness

On the Cutting Edge
Theory of Mind in Infancy

SHORT-ANSWER QUESTIONS

Upon completion of Chapter 7 you should be able to discuss the following topics. Check off those you are confident that you can discuss well. Re-read the material in the text for the topics about which you are less confident. Record the important points from your reading in the space below each topic.

1.   Explain Piaget's use of the following ideas, borrowed from biology, in his views of the structure and function of intelligence:

organization

adaptation

development

2.   Differentiate between *assimilation* and *accommodation.*

3.   Outline the four periods of development in Piaget's theory.

4.   Describe how Piaget combined naturalistic observation with experimental manipulation in his study of infants.

5.   Identify and describe the six substages of the sensorimotor period, providing the approximate ages for each substage.

6.   Summarize what Piaget's research revealed about the notion of object permanence.

7.   Explain the two general themes in Piaget's approach that are illustrated by his work on object permanence: *progressive decentering* and the importance of *invariants.*

8.   Explain how recent researchers have further investigated object permanence and summarize their findings.

9.   Discuss the findings of recent research examining the infant's physical knowledge and ability to imitate.

10.   Identify the five kinds of behaviour that Piaget described as evidence of the capacity for representational functioning emerging near the end of infancy.

11.   Discuss the strengths and limitations of preoperational thought.

12.   Explain what Piaget means by *egocentrism* in preoperational thinking. How would this be reflected in children's responses to the three-mountains problem?

13.   Explain how *centration* affects preoperational children's responses to conservation problems.

14.   Describe a typical Piagetian conservation task and discuss the differences between the responses of a preoperational and a concrete operational child.

15.   Describe the performance of the preoperational child on problems involving class inclusion, seriation, and transitivity.

16.   Summarize the major differences between preoperational and concrete operational thought.

17.   Explain what Piaget means by the concept of *operations.*

18.   Discuss what recent research has revealed concerning preoperational children's limitations in the areas of perspective taking, symbolic activity, and conservation. Is young children's thinking as deficient as Piaget claimed?

19.   Summarize the major differences between concrete operational and formal operational thought.

20.   Describe how an adolescent capable of formal operational thought would likely go about solving the pendulum problem.

21.   Discuss what recent research has revealed concerning how the tasks used by Piaget assess formal operational reasoning.

22.   State what theorists mean by *stages* of development. Summarize the three criteria that a stage theory must meet.

23.   Discuss what cross-cultural research reveals concerning the universality of Piaget's theory of cognitive development.

24.   Summarize Piaget's views of the contributions of the following four general factors to cognitive change:

biological maturation

physical experience

social experience

equilibration

25.　　Describe four principles that are often cited in discussions of Piagetian approaches to education.

26.　　Discuss the relevance of recent research on children's *concepts* to Piaget's view of the limitations of preoperational thought.

27　　Discuss what is meant by *Theory of Mind*, making reference to preoperational children's understanding of *false beliefs* and the *appearance-reality distinction*.

28.　　Explain the relevance of children's beliefs about the causes of illness to efforts to help children develop health-maintaining behaviours and cope with illness.

29.　　Discuss how the concepts of *joint attention* and *social referencing* may reveal a dawning awareness in infants of mental states.

KEY TERMS

Upon completion of Chapter 7, you should be able to define the following terms.

Cognition　　_____

_____

Sensorimotor schemes　　_____

_____

Intentional behaviour   _____

_____

Mental representation   _____

_____

Object permanence   _____

_____

A-not-B error   _____

_____

Progressive decentering   _____

_____

Egocentrism   _____

_____

Invariants   _____

_____

Symbolic function   _____

_____

Deferred imitation   _____

_____

Symbolic play   _____

_____

Qualitative identity   _____

_____

Egocentric speech   _____

_____

Centration _____

_____

Conservation _____

_____

Class inclusion _____

_____

Seriation _____

_____

Transitivity _____

_____

Operations _____

_____

Decentration _____

_____

Reversibility_____

_____

Dual representation _____

_____

Hypothetical-deductive reasoning _____

_____

Equilibration _____

_____

Equilibrium _____

_____

Concept _____

_____

Animism _____

_____

Theory of mind _____

_____

False belief _____

_____

Appearance–reality distinction _____

_____

Joint attention _____

_____

Social referencing _____

_____

FILL-IN EXERCISES

Fill in the word or words that best fit in the spaces below.

1.   Piaget's goal throughout his career was to use the study of children to answer basic philosophical questions about the nature and origins of _____.

2.   For Piaget, the essence of intelligence does not lie in individually-learned responses or isolated memories; the essence lies in the underlying _____, which takes the form of various cognitive structures that the developing child constructs.

3.   _____ occurs through the complementary processes of assimilation and accommodation.

4.   The term _____ _____ refers to the skilled and generalizable action patterns by which infants act on and makes sense of the world. They are the cognitive structures of infancy.

5.   Substage 4 of the sensorimotor period is characterized by the emergence of the first truly _____ behaviour.

6.   At substage 6 of the sensorimotor period, the infant becomes capable for the first time of mental _____.

7.   At _____ to _____ months, the infant can search systematically and intelligently for hidden objects. The infant demonstrates object _____ by searching for an object even when it is completely gone and even when it was not her own actions that made the object disappear.

8.   According to Piaget, infants begin life in a state of profound _____; that is, they literally cannot distinguish between the self and the outer world.

9.   One general conclusion from later research is that Piaget often _____-estimated infants' knowledge.

10.   The defining characteristic of the movement from sensorimotor to preoperational intelligence is the onset of _____ ability, or what Piaget called the _____ function.

11.   Near the end of infancy, babies begin to imitate models observed some time in the past, an ability that Piaget referred to as _____ imitation.

12.   When retelling a story, young children often fail to assume the perspective of their listener, acting instead as though the listener already knows everything that they know. Such story telling demonstrates _____ speech by a preoperational child.

13.   The term _____ describes the preoperational child's tendency to focus on only one aspect of a problem at a time.

14.   Understanding that if A>B and B>C, then A>C involves the ability to appreciate the _____ of quantitative relations, an ability that develops in the _____ period.

15.   The term _____ refers to the ability to order stimuli along some quantitative dimension, such as length.

16.   In the _____ operational period, children are capable of mentally manipulating abstract as well as concrete objects, events, and ideas.

17.   The child who is concerned that a piece of paper will be hurt by being cut is displaying a form of reasoning that Piaget called _____.

18.   At about 1 year of age, babies engage in social _____: looking to another for cues about how to interpret and respond to an uncertain situation.

APPLICATION

Situation

Mickey and his older brother Dave are having lunch. When their mother gives them their juice, Mickey's glass is short and fat, while Dave's is tall and thin. Although their mother is careful to pour the same amount of juice into each glass, Mickey complains that Dave got more. Their mother gets a short, fat glass from the cupboard and, while Mickey watches, pours Dave's juice from the tall, thin glass into the new short, fat one. Mickey says "That's better, now they're the same." After watching his mother pour the juice from one glass into the other, Dave just sits there chuckling. He whispers to his mother, "Boy, did you ever fool Mickey! It's the same amount of juice in both glasses!"

Questions to answer

1. Which of Piaget's stages of cognitive development most likely describes Mickey? How about Dave?

2. What does Dave realize that Mickey doesn't? What is this concept called?

3. According to Piaget's theory, what is it that causes Mickey to think there is more juice in the second glass? What is this process called?

USING WHAT YOU HAVE LEARNED

1. Deanna is a very bright young girl. When her elementary school teacher gives her class an assignment, Deanna's work always turns out to be excellent. She finishes her work quickly, usually before anyone else in the class. This leaves Deanna with free time, which she often spends talking to and distracting other students who have not yet finished their work. Based on Piaget's findings regarding the motivation necessary for cognitive growth, what advice might you give Deanna's teacher if she asked you how to best to curb her disruptive behaviour?

2. A friend's mother claims that she was unable to program the DVD player to record a favourite TV program, until it was explained to her in terms of how she usually pre-programs the microwave to cook a chicken while she is at work. How would you explain her success, in terms of the dual processes that make up the Piagetian concept of adaptation?

SAMPLE TEST QUESTIONS

1. Piaget's research has shown a consistent focus on which of the following central topics of philosophy?

    a. the child's understanding of space, time, and causality
    b. the child's understanding of number and quantity
    c. the child's understanding of classes and relations, invariance and change
    d. all of the above

2. The process by which we interpret the environment by altering our understanding to take account of new things is known as:

    a. accommodation
    b. adaptation
    c. assimilation
    d. organization

3. Piaget's third period of cognitive development is called the:

    a. preoperational period
    b. concrete operational period
    c. sensorimotor period
    d. formal operational period

4. At age 4, Derrick has a good understanding of the idea that poodles, German shepherds, bull terriers and rottweilers are all "dogs." When Derrick attends a birthday at a friend's house, he readily recognizes that his friend's cocker spaniel is also a dog. The process by which Derrick adapts to this new breed of dog best illustrates the Piagetian concept of:

    a. accommodation
    b. organization
    c. assimilation
    d. adaptation

5. Which of the following is **NOT** viewed as a weakness in Piaget's studies of infants?

    a. The studies used only a limited sample of children, all of whom were from the same family.
    b. The method involved the longitudinal study of the behaviour of the children as they developed in a natural setting.
    c. The method of study was carried out by two researchers, both of whom were parents of the children involved.
    d. b & c

6. In Piagetian theory, the first truly intentional behaviour is characteristic of which substage of the sensorimotor period?

    a. Substage 2 (one to four months)
    b. Substage 3 (four to eight months)
    c. Substage 4 (eight to twelve months)
    d. Substage 5 (twelve to eighteen months)

7. Baby Jacqueline spots her favourite toy rattle under her cat Ginger's tail. In order to retrieve her toy, Jacqueline needs first to lift the animal's tail before attempting to grasp the rattle. Jacqueline would be *unable* to perform this series of actions in which of the following substages of the sensorimotor period of development?

    a. Substage 3 (four to eight months)
    b. Substage 4 (eight to twelve months)
    c. Substage 5 (twelve to eighteen months)
    d. a & b

8. Piaget maintained that one important kind of knowledge that the child must acquire is knowledge of what it is that stays the same. For Piaget, object permanence represented the first and most basic:

    a. form of habituation
    b. conservation task
    c. cognitive invariant
    d. form of adaptation

9.   Sensorimotor schemes undergo which of the following developmental changes during the second substage (one to four months) of the sensorimotor period?

    a.   Individual schemes become progressively refined.
    b.   Individual schemes begin to be used more frequently in isolation.
    c.   Initially independent schemes begin to be coordinated.
    d.   a & c

10.   According to Piagetian research, during the first two substages of the sensorimotor period, babies:

    a.   are able to solve problems only by means of trial and error
    b.   show no evidence that they realize that objects exist apart from their own actions on them
    c.   are unable, even after a number of trials, to anticipate the re-emergence of an object they have been tracking, once it disappears behind a screen
    d.   have developed a limited number of procedures for reproducing interesting events

11.   Ten-month-old Mazen and his babysitter are sitting on the floor playing with a stuffed rabbit. Mazen's babysitter has been hiding the rabbit behind her back, and each time she has done so, Mazen has crawled around behind her and retrieved the rabbit. To make the game more interesting, Mazen's babysitter next hides the toy behind a chair. When it is Mazen's turn to look for the toy, even though he watched it being hidden behind the chair, he continues to look for the rabbit behind her back. Mazen's behaviour best illustrates Piaget's concept of:

    a.   A-not-B error   b.   accommodation
    c.   object permanence   d.   infant egocentrism

12.   In infancy, progressive decentering is manifest in:

    a.   an inability to distinguish the self from the outer world
    b.   a gradual distinguishing of self from the outer world
    c.   a tendency to focus on only one aspect of a problem at a time
    d.   a gradual willingness to share objects with others, and to engage in activities with others

13.   Which of the following is **NOT** an example of symbolic functioning in children?

    a.   A child opens her mouth prior to opening a jewellery box.
    b.   A child pretends that a plate is a flying saucer.
    c.   A child uses language.
    d.   A child sucks his thumb and the nipple of his milk bottle.

14.   Stacey loves playing hide and seek. Her favourite hiding places are under a table or behind a chair. Although her face may be hidden from view, often her bottom and legs protrude from her hiding place, in plain view. Yet Stacy believes nobody can see her. Stacey is likely in which of Piaget's periods of cognitive development?

    a.   preoperational   b.   formal operational
    c.   sensorimotor   d.   concrete operational

15. While spending a day at the beach with her family, Susan piles up and intricately decorates a large mass of sand. When Susan's father asks her what she is building, she tells him that it is the castle of a beautiful fairy princess. In Piagetian terms, Susan is engaging in:

    a. assimilation
    b. symbolic play
    c. egocentrism
    d. qualitative identity

16. In Piaget's theory, knowledge that the quantitative properties of an object or a collection of objects are not changed by a change in appearance is an achievement of:

    a. the sensorimotor period
    b. the preoperational period
    c. the concrete operational period
    d. the formal operational period

17. The term "*animism*" refers to the tendency of children to:

    a. endow inanimate objects with the qualities of life
    b. confuse their perspective with that of animals, especially pets
    c. use the term "animal" to refer to four-legged objects
    d. show confusion about whether animals can think

18. A child is presented with 13 flowers; eight of these are red roses and five are white carnations. When asked whether there are more red roses or more flowers, a concrete operational child is likely to respond:

    a. "There are more white flowers."
    b. "There are more red roses."
    c. "There are more white carnations."
    d. "There are more flowers."

19. "If Jane is older than Carol, and Carol is older than Christine, which girl is the youngest?" This type of question requires an understanding of:

    a. class inclusion
    b. conservation
    c. transitivity
    d. progressive decentering

20. Piaget's theory of formal operations has been criticized on which of the following grounds?

    a. Critics have noted that the degree of within-stage consistency is not impressive.
    b. Critics have found that responses to different formal operational tasks are only moderately correlated.
    c. Logicians have criticized the specific logical structures that Piaget believed underlie formal operational performance.
    d. all of the above

ANSWERS

FILL-IN EXERCISES

1. knowledge   2. organization   3. adaptation   4. sensorimotor schemes   5. intentional
6. representation   7. eight; twelve; permanence   8. egocentrism   9. under   10. representational; symbolic
11. deferred   12 egocentric   13. centration   14. transitivity; concrete operations   15. seriation
16. formal   17. animism   18. referencing

APPLICATION

1. Mickey is preoperational. Dave is concrete or formal operational.
2. Dave realizes that the amount of juice remains the same. *Conservation*
3. Mickey focuses only on one aspect of the glass—its height—and ignores the difference between the two glasses in width. *Centration*

SAMPLE TEST QUESTIONS

1. d	11. a
2. a	12. b
3. b	13. d
4. c	14. a
5. b	15. b
6. c	16. c
7. a	17. a
8. c	18. d
9. d	19. c
10. b	20. d

Chapter 8
Cognitive Development: The Information-Processing Approach

OUTLINE

Use this outline as you read the chapter. Enter your questions, comments, and notes in the space provided. Write down terms or statements you don't understand, with their page numbers.

THE NATURE OF THE APPROACH
Learning Objective 8.1: Define the information-processing approach and describe three methods of studying information processing.

The Flowchart Metaphor

The Computer Metaphor

Comparisons with Piaget

MEMORY IN INFANCY
Learning Objective 8.2: Explain the information-processing model of memory, and trace developmental changes in the kinds of memory

Recognition Memory

Recall Memory

MEMORY IN OLDER CHILDREN
Learning Objective 8.3: Describe how memory develops in older children and the tools that contribute to this development of memory.

The Role Of Strategies

The Role of Metamemory

The Role of Knowledge

Application
Children's Eyewitness Testimony

NUMBER
Learning Objective 8.4: Describe the development in the understanding of number from infancy to school-age.

Infants' Response to Number

Preschool Developments

Arithmetic

Focus on Research
The Inversion Principle as a Strategy for Solving Mathematics Problems

PROBLEM SOLVING
Learning Objective 8.5: Analyze the abilities and skills children use to solve applied.

The Development of Rules

Reasoning by Analogy

The Contribution of Memory to Problem Solving

Canadian Contributions
Robbie Case

COGNITIVE CHANGE
Learning Objective 8.6: Describe the mechanisms that have been proposed to account for cognitive change.

Methods of Study

SHORT-ANSWER QUESTIONS

Upon completion of Chapter 8 you should be able to discuss the following topics. Check off those you are confident that you can discuss well. Re-read the material in the text for the topics about which you are less confident. Record the important points from your reading in the space below each topic.

1.   Explain how the flowchart metaphor is used by information-processing theorists.

2.   Describe how information-processing theorists have used the computer as a useful tool on a variety of levels.

3.   How are computer simulations used to study the process of cognitive change?

4.   How does the approach known as *connectionism* model cognitive development?

5.   Discuss five issues related to cognitive change for which Siegler believes microgenetic techniques can provide valuable data.

6.   Compare and contrast the information-processing approach with the Piagetian approach.

7.   Differentiate between recognition memory and recall memory.

8.   Discuss how researchers have assessed recognition memory in infancy.

9.   Describe the developmental changes that have been found in recognition memory in infancy.

10.   Explain how researchers infer the presence of recall memory in infants.

11.   What are some explanations for the phenomenon of *infantile amnesia*?

12.   Discuss how the use of mnemonic strategies changes across age in childhood.

13.   Differentiate between a *utilization deficiency* and a *production deficiency* in strategy use.

14.   Discuss two general reasons for psychologists' interest in metamemory.

15.   Describe how constructive memory may be evident in children's recall.

16.   Discuss the issues underlying children's eyewitness testimony.

17.   Explain three ways in which expertise can affect memory.

18.   Discuss how researchers have investigated infants' sensitivity to number.

19.   Describe five principles that a counting system must honour, according to Rochel Gelman and associates. Do preschoolers understand these principles?

20.   Discuss the various strategies that children might use to solve simple addition problems. How have Siegler and colleagues assessed these strategies?

21.   What is the *inversion principle?* What do we know about preschoolers' understanding of this principle?

22.   What has research with *the dimensional-change card sort* revealed about rule-based reasoning in preschoolers?

23.   Describe Robert Siegler's investigation of children's use of rules for solving the balance scale problem.

24.   Discuss two differences in how Siegler and Piaget account for conservation of number and of quantity in children.

25.   Explain what is meant by *analogical reasoning*. When is this form of reasoning first apparent?

26.   Discuss the roles of *operating space* and *short-term storage* space in Robbie Case's theory.

27.   Describe two possible explanations for the developmental increase in short-term storage capacity.

28.   Describe and differentiate among the following four mechanisms of cognitive change:

encoding

automatization

strategy construction

strategy selection

29.   Discuss three challenges to the information-processing approach to cognitive development.

KEY TERMS

Upon completion of Chapter 8, you should be able to define the following terms.

Computer simulation   _____

_____

Connectionism _____

_____

Event Memory _____

_____

Script _____

_____

Constructive memory   _____

_____

Autobiographical memory   _____

_____

Recognition memory   _____

_____

Recall memory _____

_____

Reactivation _____

_____

Infantile amnesia   _____

_____

Mnemonic strategies   _____

_____

Utilization deficiency   _____

_____

Production deficiency   _____

_____

Study strategies _____

_____

Metamemory   _____

_____

Expertise   _____

_____

Rules   _____

_____

Executive function   _____

_____

Analogical reasoning   _____

_____

Operating space   _____

_____

Short-term storage space   _____

_____

Encoding   _____

_____

Automatization   _____

_____

Strategy construction   _____

_____

Strategy selection   _____

_____

FILL-IN EXERCISES

Fill in the word or words that best fit in the spaces below.

1.   Computer programs used by _____, in their attempts to model the human brain, take the form of artificial neural networks.

2.   As compared to the stages of development proposed by Piaget, the stages proposed by information-processing theorists are more _____ specific.

3.   The realization that some perceptually present stimulus or event has been encountered before is referred to as _____ memory.

4.   A _____ strategy is any technique that people use to help themselves remember something.

5.   The inability to remember experiences for the first two or three years of life is referred to as _____ _____.

6.   The failure to generate a mnemonic strategy spontaneously is called _____ deficiency, whereas the failure of a recently developed strategy to facilitate recall is referred to as _____ deficiency.

7.   The term _____ refers to knowledge about memory in general, and about one's own memory in particular.

8.   Flavell coined the term _____ to refer to thinking about thinking.

9.   The way in which people's general knowledge system structures and reworks the information they take in, and thus affects what they remember, is referred to as _____ _____.

10.   Piagetian research makes the point that constructive memory can operate in a _____ as well as a _____ direction.

11.   The term _____ (sometimes called *content knowledge* or *knowledge base*) refers to organized factual knowledge with respect to some content domain.

12.   _____ reasoning refers to a form of problem solving in which the solution is achieved through recognition of the similarity between the new problem and some already-understood problem.

13.   According to Robbie Case, the total problem-solving resources available to a child are divided into two components, _____ space and short-term _____ space.

14.   Four major change mechanisms have been discussed by information-processing theorists. _____ refers to attending to and forming internal representations of certain features of the environment. _____ refers to an increase in the efficiency with which cognitive operations are executed as a result of practice. _____ _____ refers to the creation of strategies for processing and remembering information. _____ _____ refers to the progressively greater use of relatively effective, in comparison to relatively ineffective, strategies.

APPLICATION

Situation

Your 14-year-old brother is distressed and comes to you for advice. In two days he will be facing his final exam in Chemistry. He has read all 12 of the required textbook chapters over once, but doesn't feel as if he knows very much.

Questions to Answer

1.   Based on what you know about mnemonic strategies, what could you tell your brother about note taking, outlining, organizing, and rehearsing the material he is studying?

2.   What could you tell your brother about metamemory that might encourage him to go beyond a single reading of the textbook chapters to prepare for the exam?

3.   How might information about the exam itself (e.g., that it consists of 100 multiple-choice questions) help you to be better able to suggest an optimal studying strategy to your brother? What would the implications of this information be in terms of recognition versus recall memory?

4.   What would you tell your brother about some of the possible benefits of self-testing prior to the exam?

USING WHAT YOU HAVE LEARNED

1. The text details the effects of constructive memory; it also presents research findings on the reliability of young children's eyewitness testimony. Based on your readings, how would you respond to a parent who is dismissing his child's claims of abuse as being attributable to a "vivid imagination."

2. A friend mentions that crying is the only way her 4-month-old baby has of getting what she wants. The friend also mentions that the baby doesn't appear able to remember things, because as soon as a toy is removed from her sight, she forgets all about it. Using the mobile that hangs over the baby's crib, how could you show this mother that her baby is capable of doing more than crying to get what she wants? (Think in terms of having the baby act on the environment in order to obtain reinforcing consequences.) How might you also demonstrate the young infant's ability to remember?

3. Not wanting your son to grow up with negative, stereotypical views about women, you tell him a bed-time story about a woman firefighter who is very strong and very brave. The next day you overhear him telling the same story to one of his stuffed animals, only this time, the firefighter in the story is a man. According to your knowledge of memory in children, how might you account for this change?

SAMPLE TEST QUESTIONS

1. Which of the following images is used to characterize the nature of the information-processing approach?

    a.   a street map   b.   a flowchart
    c.   a balance scale   d.   all of the above

2. Which method of study allows researchers to produce a continuous record of change over time, analogous to watching a movie rather than viewing a series of snapshots?

    a.   self-modifying computer simulations
    b.   microgenetic techniques
    c.   longitudinal methods
    d.   connectionism

3. One way information-processing theories differ from Piaget's theory is that

    a.   Stages referred to in information-processing theories stages tend to be more domain-specific than those described by Piaget.
    b.   Information-processing theorists are more concerned with cognitive development than was Piaget.
    c.   Information-processing theorists are more concerned with a complex system of mental rules that underlie cognitive performance than was Piaget.
    d.   all of the above

4.   Infants, 12- to 24-months of age, were shown a series of pictures of various kinds of food, then given a choice of looking at either a previously-unseen item from the food category (e.g., an apple) or an item from a new category (e.g., a chair). What were the findings of this study?

   a.   The infants looked longer at the chair than the apple, thus demonstrating that they found a new category more interesting than a familiar one.
   b.   The infants looked longer at the apple than the chair, thus demonstrating a preference for the familiar category.
   c.   The infants spent an equal amount of time looking at each, thus demonstrating their inability to distinguish by category.
   d.   The amount of time spent looking at both the apple and the chair increased as a function of the age of the infant, thus demonstrating that a child's memory improves with development.

5.   Which of the following has been found effective in increasing the duration of memory in young infants?

   a.   providing an analogy
   b.   reactivation
   c.   providing simple rules
   d.   increasing short-term storage space

6.   Which of the following cannot be considered a possible explanation for infantile amnesia?

   a.   Infant memory systems differ qualitatively from later memory systems (e.g., nonverbal vs. verbal).
   b.   Immaturity of parts of the brain in infants.
   c.   Infants do not form long-term memories.
   d.   Infants cannot share and rehearse memories within a social system.

7.   While his mother is out shopping, 12-year old Jeff receives a phone call. Although he writes nothing down, Jeff is able to relate the caller's request to his mother when she returns home a few hours later. In doing so, Jeff is using his:

   a.   metamemory   b.   recall memory
   c.   constructive memory   d.   recognition memory

8.   In one study, 3-year-olds played a memory game in which they had to keep track of a toy that had been hidden under one of several cups. Many children sat with their eyes glued to the critical cup and a finger planted firmly on it during the delay between hiding and retrieval. This act would be considered:

   a.   constructive memory
   b.   elaboration
   c.   reactivation
   d.   a rudimentary mnemonic strategy

9.   Research has found that children realize that familiar items are easier to remember than unfamiliar ones, that short lists are easier to learn than long ones, and that recognition is easier than recall. By what age does this realization generally exist in most children?

   a.   1 or 2 years
   b.   3 or 4 years
   c.   5 or 6 years
   d.   7 or 8 years

10.   When asked whether she thought it would be easier for her to remember a list of three items to buy at the store or a list of 10 items, 8-year-old Janet answered that the list of three items would be easier to remember. This illustrates Janet's:

   a.   metamemory
   b.   compliance
   c.   recognition memory
   d.   recall memory

11.   When expertise in a particular area is high, memory in that area tends to be

   a.   low, because the child's storage space is cluttered with excessive detail.
   b.   unpredictable—you have to also consider the child's content knowledge and knowledge base.
   c.   unclear—expertise and memory are not related.
   d.   high—variations in expertise contribute to variations in memory.

12.   The role of "organized factual knowledge" is stressed in contemporary information-processing accounts of memory and problem solving. This term can be used interchangeably with which of the following terms?

   a.   content knowledge
   b.   knowledge base
   c.   expertise
   d.   all of the above

13.   In one study, children viewed pictures in which sex-stereotypic activities were reversed (e.g., a girl sawing and a boy playing with dolls). On a later memory test, the children tended to report that it was the boy who did the sawing, and the girl who played with dolls. This is an example of what type of memory?

   a.   constructive memory
   b.   short-term memory
   c.   metamemory
   d.   recall memory

14.   Infants' response to number has been assessed using all of the following EXCEPT:

    a.   the habituation-dishabituation methodology
    b.   the possible-event, impossible-event procedure
    c.   conservation of quantity tasks
    d   ALL of the above have been used to assess infant response to number

15.   Children who follow Siegler's Rule 4 on the balance scale problem:

    a.   Judge the task solely in terms of the number of weights on either side, when this number is different. If the number is equal, however, they will also take distance into account.
    b.   Will be expected to solve the problem correctly in about 65% of trials.
    c.   Have mastered the weight-times-distance rule, realizing that downward force equals amount of weight multiplied by distance from the fulcrum.
    d.   Will, in Siegler's terms, have to "muddle through" in order to arrive at a solution for the problem.

16.   Which of the following is true concerning analogical reasoning?

    a.   The basic capacity for reasoning by analogy seems to be present early in life.
    b.   The ability to reason by analogy requires the abstract-reasoning abilities that emerge in adolescence.
    c.   Although analogical reasoning is evident in school-aged children, the basic capacity for this ability is not present in preschoolers.
    d.   Although some preschoolers may reason by analogy, such ability is beyond the capacity of infants.

17.   Children listened to a story in which a genie needed to transport some jewels over a wall and into a bottle. The genie solved her problem by rolling up a piece of posterboard to form a tube that she then rolled the jewels down into the bottle. The children then listened to a problem in which they were to help the Easter Bunny transport his eggs across a river and into a basket. Using aspects of the original story to solve the second problem involves:

    a.   constructive memory
    b.   reactivation
    c.   expertise
    d.   analogical reasoning

18.   According to Case's theory, short-term storage space:

    a.   can be increased through the use of mnemonic strategies
    b.   refers to the resources necessary to carry out whatever cognitive operations are being employed for the problem at hand
    c.   refers to the resources the child needs to store results from previous operations while carrying out new ones
    d.   all of the above

19.   Which of the following is **NOT** a mechanism of cognitive change discussed by information-processing theorists?

   a.   encoding
   b.   reactivation
   c.   automatization
   d.   strategy construction

20.   Which of the following is reasonably seen as a challenge to the information-processing theory of cognitive development?

   a.   the limited scope of the theory
   b.   the limited attention to the social context in which development occurs
   c.   the inability of the theory to produce a completely satisfactory explanation of how cognitive change occurs
   d.   all of the above

ANSWERS

FILL-IN EXERCISES

1. connectionists 2. domain 3. recognition 4. mnemonic 5. infantile amnesia 6. production; utilization
7. metamemory 8. metacognition 9. constructive memory 10. negative; positive 11. expertise
12. analogical 13. operating; storage 14. Encoding; Automatization; Strategy construction; Strategy selection

APPLICATION

1. All of these techniques have been found to improve recall, and you could help him develop these as effective strategies.
2. Knowledge of one's own memory is important in deciding such things as how to allocate attention, what material to study further, what the most useful encoding and recall strategies are, and so on.
3. This knowledge can relate to the types of strategies used. Multiple-choice exams mostly involve recognition memory, whereas short answer, fill-in the blanks, definitions, and essay-type exams require recall memory.
4. Self-testing is a useful study strategy to determine what has been learned and what needs to be further studied.

USING WHAT YOU HAVE LEARNED

1. Although memory involves interpretation based on the individual's general knowledge system, children can indeed give eyewitness testimony if interviewed appropriately.
2. Habituation and conditioning studies demonstrate recognition memory in young infants. Simple forms of recall also probably emerge at some time during the first year. The development of object permanence may be evidence of recall memory. Gently tie the infant's leg to the mobile with a ribbon and let him or her learn to kick to make the mobile dance. Later remove the ribbon and see if the infant continues to kick.
3. This is an example of constructive memory.

SAMPLE TEST QUESTIONS

1. b	11. d
2. b	12. d
3. a	13. a
4. a	14. c
5. b	15. c
6. c	16. a
7. b	17. d
8. d	18. c
9. c	19. b
10. a	20. d

Chapter 9
Cognitive Development:
The Sociocultural Approach

OUTLINE

Use this outline as you read the chapter. Enter your questions, comments, and notes in the space provided. Write down terms or statements you don't understand, with their page numbers.

NATURE OF THE APPROACH
Learning Objective 9.1: Describe the sociocultural approach to child development and compare and contrast it with cognitive-developmental approaches.

The Social Origins of Thought

Tools and Artifacts

The Cultural-Historical Context of Development

Comparisons with Cognitive-Developmental Theories

OBJECT EXPLORATION, TOOL USE, AND PLAY
Learning Objective 9.2: Analyze the significance of object exploration, tool use, and play within social and cultural contexts.

Exploratory and Non-symbolic Play

Symbolic Play

Implications of Symbolic Play for Development

MEMORY
Learning Objective 9.3: Describe memory development from a sociocultural perspective.
Strategies

Event Memory

Autobiographical Memory

SELF-REGULATION
Learning Objective 9.4: Describe the self-regulation involved in problem solving in the form of planning and private speech.

Planning

Private Speech

Research Classic
Training Self-Instructions as a Means of Gaining Self-Control in Impulsive Children

PEER INTERACTION AND COGNITIVE CHANGE
Learning Objective 9.5: Describe the role of peers and their effect on learning and cognitive change.

Peer Teaching

Collaboration

Peer Learning in Classrooms

Application
Scaffolding Group Discussion: The Hypothesis-Experiment-Instruction Method

CULTURAL ARTIFACTS AND MATERIAL TOOLS
Learning Objective 9.6: Analyze how cultural tools, particularly mathematical tools, shape children's thinking and problem solving.

Numeration Systems

Measurement

Currency

SHORT-ANSWER QUESTIONS

Upon completion of Chapter 9 you should be able to discuss the following topics. Check off those you are confident that you can discuss well. Re-read the material in the text for the topics about which you are less confident. Record the important points from your reading in the space below each topic.

1.   Explain Vygotsky's notion of the *Zone of Proximal Development,* describing the relevance of *scaffolding* and *guided participation* to Vygotsky's notion.

2.   Describe how tools are related to higher mental functions.

3.   Identify and describe four interrelated time frames which Vygotsky proposed should be involved in the study of development.

4.   Discuss three differences between the sociocultural approach and the Piagetian and information-processing approaches to cognitive development.

5.   Discuss the importance of object play for children's cognitive development.

6.   Describe how cultures may differ in the access children are allowed to have to objects and in parental beliefs about object play.

7.   Explain what *symbolic play* is, commenting on how it may be viewed differently by different cultures.

8.   Describe how symbolic play with siblings differs from that with mothers.

9.   Discuss how symbolic play may contribute to children's cognitive and social development.

10.   Explain how the *school cut-off design* has been used to examine the effects of schooling on memory development.

11.   Discuss what has been found concerning the influence of teachers and parents on memory strategies.

12.   Describe how children's *scripts* and "memory talk" can influence their memory.

13.   Identify two broad styles that parents use when talking about specific memories with children, and explain how these influence children's *autobiographical memory*.

14.   Discuss the ways in which children learn about and develop skills in planning.

15.   Describe how the use of private speech develops in children.

16.   Explain how Donald Meichenbaum used self-instructional training to teach impulsive children to control their behaviour.

17.   Discuss the practice of peer teaching, describing both the benefits of peer teaching as well as the various reasons why child teachers may be insensitive to learners' needs.

18.   Contrast the sociocultural view of collaboration with that of Piaget.

19.   Describe the characteristics of successful collaborations.

20.   Describe the *hypothesis-experiment-instruction* intervention used to facilitate peer learning in Japanese classrooms.

21.   Explain how both the structure of the number-naming system, as well as the speed with which the number words can be pronounced, may contribute to the superior mathematical achievement of East Asian students.

22.   Describe how children's understanding of measurement develops.

KEY TERMS

Upon completion of Chapter 9, you should be able to define the following terms.

Culture _____

_____

Zone of proximal development _____

_____

Scaffolding _____

_____

Guided participation _____

_____

Higher mental functions _____

_____

Ontogenetic development _____

_____

Microgenetic development _____

_____

Phylogenetic development _____

_____

Cultural/historical development _____

_____

Independent orientation _____

_____

Interdependent orientation   _____

_____

Replica toys   _____

_____

Imaginary companions   _____

_____

Solitary pretense   _____

_____

Sociodramatic play   _____

_____

Mediated memory   _____

_____

School cut-off design   _____

_____

Event memory   _____

_____

Script   _____

_____

Autobiographical memory   _____

_____

Private speech   _____

_____

Sociogenesis _____

_____

Socio-cognitive conflict _____

_____

Intersubjectivity _____

_____

FILL-IN EXERCISES

Fill in the word or words that best fit in the spaces below.

1.   The term _____ refers to a method of teaching in which the adult adjusts the level of help provided in relation to the child's level of performance.

2.   Barbara Rogoff coined the term _____ _____ to describe the process by which young children become competent by participating in everyday, purposeful activities under the guidance of more experienced partners.

3.   According to Vygotsky, the term _____ refers to all the means individuals have at their disposal to achieve desired goals. The most powerful of these is _____.

4.   The Piagetian and information-processing approaches focus on processes _____ to the child, such as the reorganization of cognitive structures and increased speed of processing information. Sociocultural theorists, in contrast, believe developmental change is _____ mediated.

5.   Studies have shown that early experience exploring objects _____ (*may/may not*) be essential for normal cognitive development.

6.   As would be predicted by sociocultural theory, infants spend more time exploring objects and engage in more focused and complex exploration when interacting with _____ than when playing alone.

7.   Middle-income North American culture is described as having a(n) _____ orientation, which emphasizes self-expression and personal achievement. Cultures such as Japan have a(n) _____ orientation that focuses on the individual's role within a broader social network.

8.   The most complex type of joint pretense, _____ _____, occurs when two or more people enact a variety of related roles (e.g., mother and baby; driver and passenger).

9.   Observational studies reveal that most pretend play takes place in a _____ context with other people acting as spectators or partners.

10.   Observations in Caucasian American homes suggest that children's earliest play partners are most often _____.

11.   Children _____ *(with/without)* siblings are twice as likely to demonstrate knowledge of false beliefs than those _____ *(with/without)* siblings.

12.   _____ memory involves remembering that relies on cultural tools and artifacts that support memory development and use.

13.   The _____ _____-_____ design is a research design that compares children who are close in age, but differ in school experience by one year.

14.   A _____ is a representation of the typical sequence of actions and events in some familiar context. They increase in both completeness and _____ as children develop.

15.   The term _____ _____ refers to memories that are specific, personal, and long-lasting—memories that are part of one's life-history and that have to do with the self.

16.   Researchers have identified two broad styles that parents use to elicit talk about specific memories with young children. Parents in the _____ category provide richer narrative structure than parents in the _____ category.

17.   Vygotsky referred to the process of acquiring knowledge or skills through social interactions as _____.

18.   In their attempts to scaffold others' learning, peer teachers tend more frequently to provide too _____ *(little/much)* assistance.

19.   Studies show that children begin to learn by watching peers at least by the _____ year of life.

20.   Piagetians refer to the conflict that arises during social interaction as _____ _____.

21.   From the sociocultural approach to collaboration, it matters less that partners hold divergent views on a problem than that they establish _____ —a commitment to find common ground on which to build shared understanding.

22.   In the Japanese educational intervention known as _____-_____-_____, the teacher provides three or four plausible alternatives. Students then choose one of these choices as correct, and their choices are discussed with the other students in class.

23.   The Oksapmin of Papua New Guinea use what is called a _____-_____ _____ system for counting and measuring.

24.   Research on children's measurement demonstrates the general point that children can often use tools skillfully _____ *(before/after)* they really understand them.

APPLICATION

Do you use self-guiding, private speech?

In Chapter 9, you read about the role of private speech in the control of behaviour, and how private speech becomes internalized as thought as children become older. You also learned that self-guiding private speech can be seen even in older children, when they begin a new and difficult task, with its use decreasing as they master the task.

1.   Pay close attention to your own "internalized" private speech. Can you see evidence of its self-guiding functions?

2.   Try doing an unfamiliar and complicated task (such as a puzzle, Rubik's cube, etc.). Pay close attention to your own verbalizations and self-statements. Do you see evidence of private speech?

3.   Think of a complicated task that you recently learned, such as driving. Do you remember initially guiding your behaviour through the use of private speech (e.g., "OK, now, shift into drive." "Watch that car over there!" "Got the turn-signal on?"). Did your use of private speech decline as you became more familiar with the task? Are there any situations (such as the stress of a near accident while driving) where your private speech re-emerges? [*]

USING WHAT YOU HAVE LEARNED

You've been asked by the parent-teacher association of your neighbourhood school to give a short talk on collaboration in the classroom. They ask you to talk about the following issues. What would you say?

1.   Is collaboration really that valuable?

2.   What do children learn through the process of collaboration?

3.   At what age can collaboration be introduced in school?

4.   Is it better to have friends, or classmates who are simply acquaintances, work together?

5.   Is it better to put together children who have the same understanding of a problem, or children who differ in their level of understanding?

6.   What role should the teacher play in collaborative groups?

---

[*] *To learn more about private speech and these examples, read Meichenbaum, D. (1977).* Cognitive-Behavior Modification. *Plenum Press: New York.*

SAMPLE TEST QUESTIONS

1. Vygotsky used the term "*zone of proximal development*" to describe:

    a. the distance between what a child can accomplish independently and what he/she can accomplish with the help of an adult
    b. a method of teaching in which the adult adjusts the level of help provided to the child's level of performance, the goal being to encourage independent performance
    c. the process by which young children become competent by participating in everyday, purposeful activities under the guidance of more experienced partners
    d. all of the above

2. Which of the following themes in Vygotsky's writings have proven especially influential in guiding contemporary sociocultural theory and research?

    a. Individual mental development has its origins in social sources.
    b. Human thought and action are mediated by cultural tools.
    c. The study of mental functioning requires the study of change across multiple levels.
    d. All of the above

3. Vygotsky proposed the study of development over four interrelated time frames. Development across years of an individual's life, such as childhood, is referred to as:

    a. phylogenetic development
    b. microgenetic development
    c. ontogenetic development
    d. cultural/historical development

4. How does the sociocultural view of development differ from that of Piaget?

    a. Sociocultural approaches focus on processes within the individual child, such as the reorganization of cognitive structures.
    b. Sociocultural theories view cognitive development as changes in internal mental capabilities.
    c. Sociocultural theorists do not believe that there are universal stages in children's cognitive development.
    d. Sociocultural theorists focus on speed of processing information.

5. Some scholars believe that different socialization practices are rooted in cultural conceptions of the self. Cultures that focus on the self's role within a broader social network, emphasizing interpersonal connectedness, social obligation, and conformity, are described as having a(n) _____ orientation.

    a. interpersonal   b. interdependent
    c. interconnected   d   collaborative

6.   Rebecca loves to play doctor and patient with her mother. Rebecca pretends to be the doctor, and her mother pretends to be sick or have an injury. This type of activity is referred to as

    a.   solitary pretense
    b.   sociodramatic play
    c.   solitary pretense with imaginary companions
    d.   interdependent pretense

7.   In which of the following would we expect to see more advanced play in a toddler?

    a.   Little Sarah plays alone with her stuffed animals, giving names to each.
    b.   Little Colleen plays with her two imaginary companions, "Stephie" and "Princess Mary."
    c.   Little Jennifer plays alone with replica toys that resemble real objects in a house.
    d   Little Francine plays dolls with her mother as play partner.

8.   Which of the following questions would a 4-year-old be better able to answer?

    a.   What happened yesterday?
    b.   What happened last week?
    c.   What happens at birthday parties?
    d.   What happened at Billy's birthday party yesterday?

9.   Which of the following parental styles of talking with children is more likely to improve children's autobiographical memory?

    a.   the elaborative style
    b.   the deliberative style
    c.   the attentive style
    d.   the repetitive style

10.   Which of the following is true concerning children's private speech?

    a.   Private speech decreases when children are in the presence of responsive social partners.
    b.   Private speech occurs most often on impossibly difficult tasks.
    c.   Children with learning and behaviour problems tend to rely on private speech for a longer time than their peers.
    d.   All of the above are true.

11.   Billy, who is 8 years old, is attempting to teach his classmate Dave how to solve a classification problem. What level of assistance is he most likely to offer?

    a.   Just the right amount, since the two boys are close in age.
    b.   Too little assistance.
    c.   No assistance, since Dave is likely engaged in private speech.
    d.   Too much assistance.

12.   Which of the following explanations may account for the relatively poor ability of children to scaffold the learning of other children?

    a.   Children may lack the self-regulatory skills to step back and let their partner solve the problem.
    b.   Children may lack the social-cognitive skills required for effective teaching.
    c.   The multiple demands of both solving the problem and teaching the solution to someone else may overwhelm child-teachers.
    d.   All of the above

13.   Piaget laid out three conditions necessary for cognitive change to occur when partners are collaborating. Which of the following is NOT one of those conditions?

    a.   Cognitive change occurs best when partners share a common language and system of ideas.
    b.   Cognitive change occurs best when one or both partners are unsure about their point of view, so that they can be influenced by the other partner.
    c.   Cognitive change occurs best when there is reciprocity between partners so that each feels free to express his or her own point of view.
    d.   Actually, all of the above **ARE** conditions Piaget felt were necessary for change to occur.

14.   The sociocultural approach differs from the Piagetian account of collaboration in its view of cognitive change as resulting from

    a.   cooperation and coordination
    b.   conflict and resolution
    c.   competence and motivation
    d.   argument and reconciliation

15.   One important difference between the sociocultural approach to collaboration and the Piagetian view is that

    a.   Piaget felt that even preoperational-aged children could effectively collaborate, whereas socioculturalists feel that only older children can collaborate effectively.
    b.   Piaget felt that children could not collaborate effectively until the period of concrete operations, whereas socioculturalists believe young children can collaborate effectively.
    c.   Piaget felt that collaboration was not important for children's social-cognitive development, whereas socioculturalists feel that it is.
    d.   Piaget felt that collaboration was important for children's social-cognitive development, whereas socioculturalists feel that it is not.

16.   Which of the following factors is associated with productive collaboration?

    a.   collaboration characterized by lively discussion and debate
    b.   collaborating with strangers or acquaintances
    c.   collaborations where neither partner has an advanced understanding of the problem
    d.   all of the above

17. Which of the following variables is necessary for successful whole-class instruction?

    a. Students need to come to school prepared to view their teachers as the authority.
    b. Students need to come to school prepared to teach their peers.
    c. Students need to feel comfortable making mistakes and revealing confusions in public.
    d. All of the above

18. Which of the following is NOT a factor that may contribute to the superior mathematical achievement of East Asian students over North American students?

    a. In East Asian languages, the structure of the base-10 number system is clearly represented by the structure of the number names themselves.
    b. East Asian children have larger memory spans than North American children.
    c. In East Asian languages, the number names can be pronounced more quickly than in English or French.
    d. All of the above

19. In industrialized societies, children initially

    a. pay little attention to the size of measuring units, focusing instead on the number of units counted
    b. pay little attention to the number of units counted, focusing instead on the size of the measuring units
    c. pay attention to both size and number of units
    d. focus first on size, then on number of units

20. Five-year-old Suzie is asked by her teacher to draw her own ruler and then to use it to measure. Based on what we know about children's measurement, what is Suzie most likely to do?

    a. place the numbers haphazardly on the ruler, showing no sense of order or counting
    b. show no understanding of where to begin numbering, starting with the number 3 or 4
    c. place the number 1 in correspondence with the first line on the ruler
    d. become confused between metric and non-metric units of measurement

ANSWERS

FILL-IN EXERCISES

1. scaffolding   2. guided instruction   3. tools; language   4. internal; socially   5. may not
6. caregivers   7. independent; interdependent   8. sociodramatic play   9. social
10. the mother   11. with; without   12. mediated   13. school cut-off   14. script; complexity
15. autobiographical memory   16. elaborative; repetitive   17. sociogenesis   18. much
19. second   20. sociocognitive conflict   21. intersubjectivity   22. hypothesis-experiment-instruction
23. body-part enumeration   24. before

USING WHAT YOU HAVE LEARNED

1. Collaboration may promote long-term conceptual change.

2. Children encounter differences of opinion and divergent views through collaboration.

3. There is some evidence that collaboration can be introduced as early as the preschool years.

4. Collaboration among friends appears more successful than among children who are simply acquaintances.

5. Collaboration is more successful when one partner has a more advanced understanding of a problem than when neither understands it well.

6. Teachers can model appropriate discourse and scaffold student discussions.

SAMPLE TEST QUESTIONS

1. a	11. d
2. d	12. d
3. c	13. b
4. c	14. a
5. b	15. b
6. b	16. a
7. d	17. c
8. c	18. b
9. a	19. a
10. c	20. c

Chapter 10
Intelligence and Schooling

OUTLINE

Use this outline as you read the chapter. Enter your questions, comments, and notes in the space provided. Write down terms or statements you don't understand, with their page numbers.

THE NATURE OF IQ TESTS
Learning Objective 10.1: Explain how intelligence traditionally is defined and measured.

The Binet Approach to Measuring Intelligence

Other Tests of Childhood Intelligence

Evaluating the Tests

ISSUES IN THE STUDY OF INTELLIGENCE
Learning Objective 10.2: Understand the organization and stability of intelligence, and the origins of individual differences.
Organization of Intelligence

Stability of IQ

Origins of Individual Differences

CONTRIBUTIONS OF THE ENVIRONMENT
Learning Objective 10.3: Understand the ways in which the environment affects IQ.

Longitudinal Studies

Research with the HOME

Families and Achievement: Cross-Cultural Research

Ethnicity, Environment, and IQ Scores

Early Intervention Programs

Conclusions from Early Intervention Programs

Application
Reducing Stereotype Threat in Minority Populations

SCHOOLING: VARIATIONS AND EFFECTS
Learning Objective 10.4: Evaluate different aspects of the schooling experience and how these affect cognitive development.

Cross-Cultural Studies

Amount of Schooling

Quality of Schooling

Contextual Contributors to Schooling

Research Classic
Pygmalion in the Classroom

ALTERNATIVE CONCEPTIONS OF INTELLIGENCE
Learning Objective 10.5: Identify alternative conceptions of intelligence

Evolutionary Approaches

Dynamic Testing

Gardner's Multiple Intelligences

Giftedness and Creativity

SHORT-ANSWER QUESTIONS

Upon completion of Chapter 10 you should be able to discuss the following topics. Check off those you are confident that you can discuss well. Re-read the material in the text for the topics about which you are less confident. Record the important points from your reading in the space below each topic.

1.   Summarize the important differences between the psychometric approach and the Piagetian, information-processing, and sociocultural perspectives.

2.   Describe the origin and content of the Stanford-Binet intelligence test.

3.   Describe how the Wechsler tests (the WISC-IV and the WPPSI) assess childhood intelligence and explain how they differ from the Stanford-Binet.

4.   Describe the advantages of the Kaufman Assessment Battery for Children (K-ABC).

5.   Distinguish between the concepts of test reliability and validity.

6.   Describe the relationship between IQ and academic performance.

7.   Discuss the "general versus specific" question concerning the organization of intelligence.

8.   Discuss the relationship between infant intelligence and later intelligence. How may "response to novelty" link intelligence in infancy and childhood?

9.   Summarize two rules for predicting the stability of IQ across childhood.

10.   Summarize the general findings of family studies, adoption studies, and twin studies concerning the origins of individual differences in intelligence.

11.   Explain the concept of *heritability*. What are the limitations of the heritability statistic?

12.   Describe the HOME instrument and discuss the findings of research using it .

13.   Compare how Canadian and American students perform on tests of mathematics achievement.

14.   Discuss how environment, experience, and motivational factors can contribute to inter-group differences in IQ scores.

15.   Describe two Canadian and two American early intervention projects, highlighting their similarities and differences.

16.   Outline the major conclusions that can be drawn from the findings of early intervention programs.

17.   Discuss how *stereotype threat* influences test performance. How can this influence be reduced?

18.   Discuss how schooling may affect cognitive development.

19.   Explain how amount of schooling is related to IQ. Is there evidence for a cause-effect direction to this relationship?

20.   Differentiate factors that do and do not influence school success according to Michael Rutter's research.

21.   Discuss the pros and cons of the practice of *ability grouping*.

22.   Discuss two general kinds of evidence that support Eccles' argument that the typical middle school or junior high provides a poor *stage-environment* fit for young adolescents.

23.   Explain the importance of peers, parents, and general cultural background to success at school.

24.   Describe how Rosenthal and Jacobson assessed the effects of teacher expectations. What were the conclusions of their study?

25.   Explain how evolutionary psychologists conceptualize intelligence, differentiating between *biologically primary abilities* and *biologically secondary abilities*.

26.   Explain what *dynamic assessment* refers to, discussing how such procedures differ from traditional IQ assessments.

27.   Discuss how Howard Gardner's theory of multiple intelligences differs from more traditional approaches to intelligence. What are the eight distinct intelligences proposed by Gardner?

28.   Discuss the relationship between IQ and giftedness. What characteristics other than high IQ characterize gifted children?

29.   Contrast *convergent thinking* and *divergent thinking*. How do these styles of thinking relate to creativity?

KEY TERMS

Upon completion of Chapter 10, you should be able to define the following terms.

Psychometric   _____

_____

Reliability   _____

_____

Validity _____

_____

g   _____

_____

Hierarchical model of intelligence   _____

_____

Heritability   _____

_____

Flynn effect   _____

_____

HOME _____

_____

Stereotype threat   _____

_____

Ability grouping _____

_____

Stage-environment fit   _____

_____

Cultural compatibility hypothesis _____

_____

Environment of evolutionary adaptiveness _____

_____

Biologically primary abilities   _____

_____

Biologically secondary abilities _____

_____

Dynamic assessment   _____

_____

Convergent thinking   _____

_____

Divergent thinking   _____

_____

FILL-IN EXERCISES

Fill in the word or words that best fit in the spaces below.

1. The first successful intelligence test was developed in Paris in 1905 by Alfred _____ and Theodore _____.

2. The ability to predict _____ success was the prime criterion for an item's inclusion in the first intelligence test.

3. The Stanford-Binet test is a direct descendent of the original intelligence test developed in Paris. It was developed in 1916 by _____ at Stanford University.

4. There is no absolute metric for measuring intelligence, such as there is for measuring height or weight. Instead, a child's IQ is a function of how that child's performance _____ with the performance of other children the same age.

5. The accuracy with which a measuring instrument assesses the attribute that it is designed to measure is referred to as its _____.

6. To determine the structure of intelligence, psychometric researchers use a statistical procedure called _____ _____ to make sense of the pattern of correlations across different measures of intelligence.

7. Spearman proposed a two-factor theory of intelligence: factor _____ refers to general intelligence, while _____ refers to abilities that contribute to performance on particular tasks.

8. A number of researchers have suggested that the common thread linking intelligence in infancy to intelligence in childhood may be an individual's response to _____.

9. The Fagan Test of Infant Intelligence measures how long infants look at _____ as compared to _____ pictures.

10.   Results of adoption studies reveal that typically the adopted child's IQ correlates more strongly with the IQs of the _____ *(biological/adoptive)* parents than with the IQs of the _____ *(biological/adoptive)* parents.

11.   The most widely accepted contemporary estimates of the heritability of IQ place the value (i.e., its *heritability index*) at _____ to _____.

12.   The _____ Effect refers to an increase over time in the average level of performance on IQ tests.

13.   _____ _____ is the extra pressure that people feel in situations in which their performance may confirm a negative expectation about their group.

14.   _____ _____ is the practice of separating students into groups of similar ability for purposes of instruction.

15.   According to the notion of _____-_____ fit, development proceeds most smoothly when the environmental opportunities and challenges during a particular time period match the capacities and needs of the developing child.

16.   Geary uses the term biologically _____ abilities to refer to abilities shaped by natural selection to solve recurring problems faced by ancestral humans.

17.   Studies using the _____ _____ procedure have confirmed Vygotsky's claim that IQ tests provide an incomplete picture of children's intelligence.

18.   Howard Gardner argues that humans possess at least _____ relatively distinct intelligences.

19.   _____ thinking is "right-answer-oriented" thinking—the form of thought emphasized on IQ tests.

20.   Most contemporary accounts of creativity can be labelled _____ theories, in that they stress the coming together of multiple contributors that must work together to make creativity possible.

APPLICATION

Situation

Andrea and Mark have just experienced the delivery of their first child—a baby boy. After a standard period of maternity leave, Andrea will be returning to her full-time job as a chemist. Since Mark is required to work long hours at his accounting firm, the couple has arranged for a babysitter to come into their home during the day once Andrea returns to work. Still, the couple is very concerned about baby Alex's intellectual development. From their past experience with friends who have children, it seems that the children of stay-at-home mothers develop more quickly and end up being the most competent performers at school. This leads them to suspect that the amount of time parents spend with their children is a critical factor in children's intellectual development.

Questions to Answer

1. Based on your knowledge of research on the home environment as a context within which a child's intellectual skills develop, is there any evidence to suggest that the total amount of time spent with a child is a critical determinant of a child's intellectual development?

2. What suggestions might you make to Andrea and Mark in order for them to create a home environment that will be maximally beneficial to Alex's intellectual development? What role can they play in determining the kinds of experiences he has, even when they're not interacting with him?

3. What recommendations would you make to Andrea and Mark concerning how they should interact with Alex when they are with him?

4. Upon checking with the babysitter, Andrea learns that Alex is quite happy to play with one or two favourite toys in his playpen most of the day. The babysitter is generally pleased to leave him there, because if he were allowed to wander freely he might break something. How should Andrea respond?

5. Being first-time parents, Andrea and Mark are uncertain about the extent that they will eventually need to discipline Alex. From your reading of Chapter 10 concerning the relation between parental discipline and children's IQ, what would you suggest to these parents?

USING WHAT YOU HAVE LEARNED

1. A researcher investigating the heritability of IQ in a sample of 15 year-old English-speaking Hawaiian children finds the heritability in this sample to be .60. What expectations would this finding impose if the same researcher later investigated the heritability of IQ in a sample of French-speaking Canadian children of the same age?

2. You are discussing the relatively-poor mathematics performance of American children as compared to that of children from China and Japan. A friend asserts that the blame for this difference rests squarely on the American school system. How would you respond? Are there other factors that should be considered? How do Canadian children compare on tests of mathematics?

3. You see on an afternoon television talk show an "expert" commenting on the issue of racial/ethnic differences in IQ. This individual argues that there are racial differences in IQ and that they are clearly genetic in origin. A second expert then presents a countervailing position. How would this second expert counter the first expert's genetic position?

SAMPLE TEST QUESTIONS

1.   The Stanford-Binet test of intelligence:

    a.   is a direct historical descendant of the original Binet-Simon test
    b.   has been revised several times since it was first developed in 1916
    c.   is a test of childhood intelligence that is applicable to every age group within the span of childhood, except infancy
    d.   all of the above

2.   Which of the following general abilities is the current version of the Stanford-Binet intelligence test **NOT** intended to assess?

    a.   divergent thinking
    b.   verbal reasoning
    c.   quantitative reasoning
    d.   fluid reasoning

3.   One difference between the WISC-IV and the Stanford-Binet is that:

    a.   the WISC-IV includes an explicit attempt at cultural diversity and cultural fairness
    b.   the WISC-IV has a grounding in information-processing conceptions of intelligence
    c.   the WISC-IV measures sequential processing as well as simultaneous processing
    d.   the WISC-IV is divided into four scales assessing different aspects of intellectual performance

4.   Louis Thurstone argued for a differentiated model of intelligence. The intelligence test he developed was designed to assess how many "primary mental abilities"?

    a.   one
    b.   six
    c.   seven
    d.   two

5.   In the earliest attempts to predict later intelligence from scores on infancy IQ tests, the first conclusion was that traditional tests of infant intelligence:

    a.   did not relate well to later intelligence test scores
    b.   related very well to later intelligence test scores
    c.   related to later intelligence test scores partially for female subjects, but not at all for males
    d.   were not of any use at all

6. One of the main findings to emerge from adoption studies concerns the pattern of correlations in parent and child IQ. Typically, the adopted child's IQ:

   a. correlates more strongly with the IQs of the adoptive parents than with the IQs of the biological parents
   b. correlates more strongly with the IQs of the biological parents than with the IQs of the adoptive parents
   c. does not correlate with the IQs of the biological parents in cases where the child was adopted shortly after at birth
   d. correlates more strongly with the IQ of the adoptive mother than of the adoptive father

7. A researcher studying children who have been adopted at birth finds that in her sample of 100 adopted children, the majority have above-average IQs, falling in the 105 to 110 range. What is likely the most plausible explanation for this finding?

   a. Adoptive parents tend to be highly-motivated parents, and adoptive homes tend to be privileged in various ways.
   b. By chance, this researcher happened to test a sample of children with an average IQ that was unusually high compared to that of the population as a whole.
   c. Children who are adopted tend to work extremely hard in school and stay in school longer than children who are not adopted. This contributes to their acquisition of the specific skills and the specific kinds of knowledge that IQ tests measure.
   d. All of the above are equally plausible explanations for this finding.

8. The term "*heritability*" refers to:

   a. the proportion of variance in a trait that can be attributed to genetic variance in the sample being studied
   b. the degree to which adopted children's IQ correlates with the IQs of their adoptive parents
   c. an estimate of the extent to which differences among people come from differences in their genes as opposed to differences in their environments
   d. both a & c

9. Which of the following is supported by studies using the HOME instrument?

   a. There is a strong genetic component to intelligence.
   b. The quality of the child's home environment is predictive of later IQ.
   c. Home environments are not really related to IQ.
   d. Home environments are related to only to certain aspects of intelligence.

10. A researcher assesses divergent thinking in pairs of twins. She finds that in identical twins, the correlation between their scores is .61, while in fraternal twins it is .50. Using the *heritability index* described in the text, what is your estimate of the heritability of divergent thinking in this sample?

   a. 1.11   b. .06   c. .22   d. .11

11.   Schools as well as homes can affect children's intellectual development. Cross-cultural studies indicate that schooling promotes which of the following cognitive skills?

      a.   classification
      b.   metacognition
      c.   memory
      d.   all of the above

12.   On which of the following tasks would you expect Joanne, who has been to school, to outperform Rheta, who has not?

      a.   recognizing that a piece of play-dough that is rolled into a big, round ball, and one that is rolled out into a long, skinny string, actually have the same mass
      b.   remembering a list of 10 items to buy at the store by repeating the list of items to herself over and over again
      c.   realizing that a half-cup of water maintains the same volume, whether it is left in a large, shallow bowl, or poured into a tall, narrow wine glass
      d.   all of the above

13.   It has long been known that there is a positive relation between number of years of education completed and IQ score. In explaining this, Stephen Ceci has argued that:

      a.   schooling may actually increase IQ
      b.   IQ tests are overrated as predictors of school performance
      c.   IQ tests are not valid measures of intelligence
      d.   IQ tests do not predict school performance

14.   Participation in an early intervention program is generally associated with:

      a.   higher scores on standardized achievement tests
      b.   lower probability of being assigned to special education classes
      c.   lower probability of being retained in a grade
      d.   all of the above

15.   Which of the following is **NOT** a documented positive effect of participation in the well-known intervention program, Project Head Start?

      a.   greater success in school
      b.   improvements in children's IQs lasting until adolescence
      c.   better health status
      d.   a and b

16.   Early intervention programs that provide more comprehensive services and use multiple routes are more effective than programs that do not. This corresponds to which of Ramey and Ramey's (1998) six principles of successful intervention?

    a.   Principle of program intensity
    b.   Principle of direct provision of learning experiences
    c.   Principle of program breadth and flexibility
    d.   Principle of environmental maintenance of development

17.   Which of the following is among the factors found by Rutter to influence school success?

    a.   the financial and physical resources available to the school
    b.   opportunities for students to participate in school-related activities
    c.   overall size of the school
    d.   all of the above

18.   Howard Gardner's approach to intelligence emphasizes:

    a.   application of g to many contexts of human behaviour
    b.   the use of factor analysis to determine the structure of intelligence
    c.   distinct, multiple intelligences accounting for ability in different domains
    d.   the primary importance of linguistic intelligence

19.   According to Geary's evolutionary approach, skills such as reading and higher mathematics are called:

    a.   biologically secondary abilities
    b.   biologically based abilities
    c.   biologically prized abilities
    d.   biologically inherited abilities

20.   When asked what she could use a newspaper for, Sarah says: "Well, you could read it. Then, you could make paper dolls out of it. You could also roll it up and use it like a vase to put flowers in. You could also use it like wallpaper to decorate your room. You could put it under your coat to keep warm. You can also use it for hamster litter. You could even cut it into small pieces and put it in the garden soil to help fertilize your plants." Sarah's thinking would be described as:

    a.   means-end thinking
    b.   inappropriate thinking
    c.   divergent thinking
    d   dynamic thinking

ANSWERS

FILL-IN EXERCISES

1. Binet; Simon   2. academic   3. Lewis Terman   4. compares   5. validity   6. factor analysis
7. *g*; *s*   8. novelty   9. novel; familiar   10. biological; adoptive   11. .4 to .7   12. Flynn   13. stereotype threat
14. ability grouping   15. stage-environment   16. primary   17. dynamic assessment   18. eight
19. convergent   20. confluence

APPLICATION

1. The issue is more complex than just amount of time. Parental involvement with the child, including responsiveness, providing the opportunity for daily stimulation, and so on, is important.
2. Organize the physical and temporal environment; provide opportunities for the child to do things outside of the home; provide appropriate play materials; provide opportunities for variety.
3. Be emotionally and verbally responsive and involved.
4. It would be better to provide variety in toys and experiences. Take him out of the play pen and take him places, provide some new and interesting toys, interact with him, read to him, and so on.
5. Hostility, scolding, derogating, and excessive physical punishment should be avoided.

USING WHAT YOU HAVE LEARNED

1. The value of the heritability statistic is specific to the sample being studied. Thus knowing its value in one sample tells us little about its value in a different sample.
2. The school system likely plays a role. However, there are also demonstrated cultural differences in how families encourage and respond to their children's academic performance that may contribute to this effect. Recent data indicate that Canadian children from all provinces perform quite well on mathematics.
3.The second expert would point to the folly of applying heritability estimates from one sample to another and would emphasize the importance of taking into account environmental, experiential, and motivational differences that may exist between groups.

SAMPLE TEST QUESTIONS

1. d	11. d
2. a	12. b
3. d	13. a
4. c	14. d
5. a	15. b
6. b	16. c
7. a	17. b
8. d	18. c
9. b	19. a
10. c	20. c

Chapter 11
Language Development

OUTLINE

Use this outline as you read the chapter. Enter your questions, comments, and notes in the space provided. Write down terms or statements you don't understand, with their page numbers.

THEORIES OF LANGUAGE DEVELOPMENT
Learning Objective 11.1: Compare and contrast four major theories of language development.

Nativist Theory

Environmental/Learning Approaches

Cognitive-Developmental Models

Sociocultural Approaches

THE PREVERBAL PERIOD
Learning Objective 11.2: Trace the developments in the first year of life that establish the preverbal basis for language learning.

Speech Perception

Listening Preferences

Early Sounds

Gestures and Nonverbal Responses

Transition to Words

SEMANTICS
Learning Objective 11.3: Describe the processes by which children first use words and develop vocabulary.

Early Lexical Development

Mechanisms of Semantic Development

GRAMMAR
Learning Objective 11.4: Describe the processes by which children learn to communicate grammatically.

Development of Grammar

Research Classic
Adding Endings to "Wugs" and Things

Mechanisms of Grammar Acquisition

On the Cutting Edge
Is Language Separate from General Cognitive Ability? The Message from Williams Syndrome

PRAGMATICS
Learning Objective 11.5: Describe the means by which children learn the pragmatics of language use.

Speech Acts

Discourse

Social Referential Communication

Application
Language Differences in School: Teaching (and Learning) One Language or Two?

Focus on Research
French Immersion in Canadian Schools

SHORT-ANSWER QUESTIONS

Upon completion of Chapter 11 you should be able to discuss the following topics. Check off those you are confident that you can discuss well. Re-read the material in the text for the topics about which you are less confident. Record the important points from your reading in the space below each topic.

1.   Discuss the basic principles of the following four theoretical approaches to language acquisition:

nativist theory

environmental/learning approaches

cognitive-developmental models

sociocultural approaches

2.   Describe preverbal receptive language abilities and preferences in infants.

3.   Outline and discuss the importance of the development of expressive language abilities in infants (i.e., early sounds and gestures).

4.   Describe deficits in the language development of deaf babies.

5.   Explain the differences between a *referential style* and an *expressive style* of lexical development. How do biology and environment interact to produce these two styles?

6.   Describe the nature of children's early words, focusing on the following characteristics of early word use:

overextensions

underextensions

coining

holophrases

7. Explain how grammatical cues contribute to semantic development. Why is this process called *syntactic bootstrapping*?

8. Explain how *lexical contrast theory* and the *principle of mutual exclusivity* act as constraints permitting children to acquire the meanings of new words quickly.

9. Discuss how parents contribute to children's semantic development.

10. Describe the development of grammar as children move from single-word to more sentence-like communications.

11. Explain what *overregularization* involves. Differentiate this term from the term *overextension*, discussed earlier.

12. Explain what is meant by *semantic bootstrapping*. Differentiate this term from *syntactic bootstrapping*, discussed earlier.

13. Describe how the notion of o*perating principles* explains grammar acquisition.

14.   Describe the strategies for acquiring grammar proposed by the *competition model*.

15.   Discuss the role parents play in grammar acquisition. Is *infant-directed speech* important? Explain each of the following parental responses: expansions, recasts, and clarification questions.

16.   Discuss how Williams syndrome may provide evidence for the nativist view of language.

17.   Explain what is meant by "rules of discourse," and how such rules are important for conversation.

18.   Discuss how speaker skills and listener skills are important for social referential communication.

19.   Discuss the one- versus two-language hypotheses concerning how bilingual children approach the task of learning two languages.

20.   Discuss the effectiveness of French immersion with reference to children's French proficiency, their competence in English, and their appreciation of Francophone Canadians and their culture.

KEY TERMS

Upon completion of Chapter 11, you should be able to define the following terms.

Productivity _____

_____

Nativist theory _____

_____

Surface structure _____

_____

Deep structure _____

_____

Language acquisition device (LAD) _____

_____

Transformational grammar _____

_____

Infant-directed speech _____

_____

Language acquisition support system (LASS) _____

_____

Phonology _____

_____

Phoneme _____

_____

Categorical perception _____

_____

Cooing _____

_____

Reduplicated babbling _____

_____

Babbling drift _____

_____

Semantics _____

_____

Lexicon _____

_____

Naming explosion _____

_____

Referential style_____

_____

Expressive style_____

_____

Overextensions _____

_____

Underextensions _____

_____

Coining _____

_____

Holophrase _____

_____

Syntactic bootstrapping _____

_____

Fast-mapping _____

_____

Constraints _____

_____

Lexical contrast theory _____

_____

Principle of mutual exclusivity _____

_____

Grammar _____

_____

Syntax _____

_____

Inflections _____

_____

Telegraphic speech _____

_____

Overregularization   _____

_____

Semantic bootstrapping _____

_____

Operating principles   _____

_____

Language-making capacity (LMC)   _____

_____

Competition model   _____

_____

Expansion   _____

_____

Recasts_____

_____

Clarification questions   _____

_____

Pragmatics   _____

_____

Speech act   _____

_____

Discourse   _____

_____

Social referential communication   _____

_____

FILL-IN EXERCISES

Fill in the word or words that best fit in the spaces below.

1.   Chomsky's psycholinguistic model proposed that the brain contains a speech-analyzing
         mechanism, referred to as the _____ _____ _____.

2.   Structured social interactions or "routines" taking place between infants and their mothers, that are
         central to the language acquisition support system (LASS), are referred to as _____.

3.   The term _____ refers to contrasts in speech sounds that change the meaning of what is heard.

4.   By _____ _____ of age, infants seem to lose a good deal of their ability to discriminate sound
         contrasts to which they have not been exposed.

5.   At about 2 months of age, infants begin to produce one-syllable vowel sounds known as _____.

6.   At about _____ months of age, reduplicated babbling occurs.

7.   Infants first begin to use gestural responses for communication at about _____ to _____
         months of age.

8.   Gestures in infants may serve a referential communication function. Initially, this form of behaviour
         involves _____, where babies hold up objects for an adult's acknowledgment. These gestures
         may then evolve into _____, and eventually into _____ and _____.

9.   By the age of 18 months, average children possess a lexicon of about _____ spoken words, and
         about _____ words that they understand.

10.   Children who display a _____ style produce a large proportion of nouns and object labels,
         whereas those who display a _____ style place a greater emphasis on language as a pragmatic
         tool for expressing needs and for social interaction.

11.   Overextensions and underextensions both characterize word learning. Although less common in
         production, _____ *(overextensions/underextensions)* are frequent in comprehension.

12.   When confronted with an object for which they do not know the name, children sometimes
         overextend the label of a similar object. Alternatively, they may deal with gaps in their vocabulary
         by creating new words, a process called _____.

13.   A _____ is a single word sentence used to express a larger idea. It is common during the second year of life.

14.   Children as young as 3 can sometimes acquire at least a partial meaning of a word after only one exposure to it, a process called _____-_____.

15.   According to _____ _____ theory, when children hear an unfamiliar word they automatically assume the new word has a different meaning from that of any word they already know.

16.   The principle of _____ _____ states that children believe that objects can only have one name.

17.   _____ are certain endings added to words that modify the meanings of words.

18.   The aspect of grammar that involves word order is referred to as _____.

19.   When children apply the rules to every noun or verb, including exceptions, they make an error known as _____.

20.   _____ _____ refers to a proposed mechanism of grammatical development in which children use semantic cues to infer aspects of grammar.

21.   Slobin developed a model of the child's language-making capacity (LMC) that includes more than 40 _____ principles.

22.   Repeating a child's incorrect statement in a corrected or more complete form is referred to as _____, whereas restating the child's remark using a different structure is called _____.

23.   The belief that children continually strive to find better ways of communicating their needs or desires has led to the study of the social uses of language, referred to as _____.

24.   Social _____ communication is a form of communication in which a speaker sends a message in such a way that the listener understands it.

USING WHAT YOU HAVE LEARNED

People who are unfamiliar with normal language development often misinterpret the normal phases of language development that children go through as a sign either that a child is extremely advanced linguistically, or of a problem in the child's language development. Below are some examples of how some parents might misinterpret the language of their children. From what you have read in Chapter 11, identify what language phenomenon the parent is actually describing, and think about how you would correct the parent's misconception.

1. "I think I may have a genius on my hands! Little Billy is only six months old, and already he's said his first word. Yesterday he said 'da-da.' To think his first word was daddy! Today he didn't get it quite right, he said 'da-da-da,' but I'm sure that was just a mistake. Just think, his first word at six months!"

2. "Kim seems to be losing what she had. She used to say things correctly, but now she makes all kinds of mistakes. Like, just yesterday she said 'I breaked it,' when she used to say 'broke.' The other day she said 'my foots' when she used to say 'my feet.' I wonder if the other kids at the daycare are a bad influence on her?"

3. "I'm not sure what's wrong with little Lise. She can't tell the difference between a dog, a cat, and even a squirrel. She calls cats and squirrels 'doggie.' I'm worried she may have some kind of vision problem."

4. "Little Raoul sure has some weird ideas. Yesterday we went to the pet store and looked at the fish. He has a goldfish at home. When I told him that these sure were pretty fish at the pet store, he said 'No!, Them not fish, fish at home!' Does he really think he's the only one who has a fish?"

5. "Carol doesn't seem to want to learn new words. All she does is use words she already has. The other day, she saw a kiwi-fruit and instead of asking what it was, she said 'that's the fuzzy-egg.' Will she ever learn any new words?"

APPLICATION

Try to get a chance to observe people talking with young children. Pay close attention to "how" they talk.

1.   Can you see signs of infant-directed speech? What characteristics do you notice?

2.   Is infant-directed speech only used by mothers? Do fathers use it? How about other children?

3.   If you have the opportunity, try to observe people who differ in how accustomed they are to interacting with young children. Are there differences in how they talk to children? Does using infant-directed speech seem related to a person's familiarity with young children?

4.   Some skeptics argue that there is nothing special about the way adults talk to young children. They argue that characteristics of infant-directed speech can be seen in other interactions, even those that don't involve talking to children. Can you see evidence of this (e.g., pet owners talking to dogs, children talking to toys)? Why would people use such a style of talking? Is this necessarily evidence against the notion of infant-directed speech?

SAMPLE TEST QUESTIONS

1.   Chomsky's views of language acquisition challenged _____ theory, a theory that previously had been generally accepted by psychologists.

    a.   Bandura's
    b.   Bruner's
    c.   Piaget's
    d.   Skinner's

2   "Surface structure" refers to:

    a.   a hypothetical structure, located on the surface of the brain, that analyzes speech input
    b.   inborn knowledge humans have about the properties of any language system
    c.   the structured context that parents provide for language learning
    d.   the way words and phrases are arranged in spoken languages

3   The language acquisition support system (LASS) is an important concept in which view of language acquisition?

    a.   psycholinguistic
    b.   sociocultural
    c.   cognitive-developmental
    d.   ethological

4.   The notion that children use their early cognitive concepts to extract rules of language from the speech they hear is associated with which approach to language acquisition?

a.   psycholinguistic
b.   cognitive-developmental
c.   learning-based approach
d.   sociocultural

5.   "Cooing" consists of:

a.   identical sounds, strung together
b.   gestures and nonverbal responses
c.   a single word used to express a larger idea
d.   one-syllable vowel sounds

6.   At around six months of age, babies begin to string together several identical sounds, to produce what is described as:

a.   cooing
b.   reduplicated babbling
c.   holophrases
d.   telegraphic speech

7.   The hypothesis that the sounds infants make while babbling become increasingly similar to those they are hearing in the language around them is known as:

a.   babbling drift
b.   reduplicated babbling
c.   naming explosion
d.   referential style

8.   Infants begin to use gestures as a form of *referential communication* at around:

a.   4–5 months of age
b.   6–7 months of age
c.   8–9 months of age
d.   11–12 months of age

9.   Which of the following gestural responses tends to emerge first in young children's communication?

a.   requesting
b.   pointing
c.   labelling
d.   showing

10.   Some children produce a very large proportion of nouns, especially object names, and use language primarily to label things. This style is referred to as:

    a.   expressive
    b.   referential
    c.   overextensive
    d.   expansive

11.   A child points to a rake and says "that's the grass-comb." This is an example of:

    a.   overextension
    b.   expansion
    c.   coining
    d.   overregularization

12.   Little Sarah says "Ball!" and points to her favourite ball. Her parents have figured out that when she says this, she is expressing the entire sentence "I want the ball!" This is an example of:

    a.   a holophrase
    b.   an operating principle
    c.   telegraphic speech
    d.   an overextension

13.   Little Phil was given a toonie by his grandfather. He calls it "cookie." This is an example of:

    a.   coining
    b.   overregularization
    c.   overextension
    d.   underextension

14.   Little Melanie told her dad "I brushed my teeths, daddy, because I eated too much candies." This sentence contains examples of:

    a.   coining
    b.   overregularization
    c.   telegraphic speech
    d.   overextension

15.   Two-year-old Gail has a pet poodle. The other day, her uncle said "That's a nice poodle you have there, Gail." Little Gail began crying, and said "Not poodle, him dog!" Gail's response is best explained by the:

    a.   semantic bootstrapping explanation
    b.   competition model
    c.   lexical contrast theory
    d.   principle of mutual exclusivity

16. The grammar in little Gail's statement in question 15 illustrates:

    a. a holophrase
    b. overregularization
    c. telegraphic speech
    d. an operating principle

17. Which of the following is **NOT** a characteristic of *"infant-directed speech?"*

    a. short utterances spoken slowly
    b. frequent grammatical errors
    c. repetition and frequent labelling
    d. focus on the here-and-now

18. When mothers respond to their children's ill-formed statements by repeating the incorrect statement in a corrected or more complete form, this form of feedback is referred to as:

    a. recasting
    b. a clarification question
    c. expansion
    d. selective imitation

19. The belief that children acquire language because it provides them with a powerful tool for communicating with others and achieving their goals is characteristic of which approach?

    a. sociocultural approach
    b. cognitive-developmental approach
    c. nativist approach
    d. social-learning approach

20. Which of the following is **NOT** true about bilingual children?

    a. Bilingual children have been found to be more advanced than monolinguals in some areas of cognition.
    b. Younger bilingual children frequently mix or combine forms of the two languages within the same utterance.
    c. Children in bilingual homes initially acquire both languages more slowly than children in monolingual homes.
    d. Having to simultaneously learn two languages results in cognitive deficits associated with the slower growth of language skills.

ANSWERS

FILL-IN EXERCISES

1. language acquisition device   2. formats   3. phoneme   4. one year   5. cooing   6. six   7. eight; ten
8. showing; giving; pointing, labelling   9. 100; 200   10. referential; expressive   11. underextensions
12. coining   13. holophrase   14. fast-mapping   15. lexical contrast   16. mutual exclusivity
17. Inflections   18. syntax   19. overregularization   20. semantic bootstrapping   21. operating
22. expansion; recasting   23. pragmatics   24. referential

USING WHAT YOU HAVE LEARNED

1. reduplicated babbling
2. overregularization
3. overextension
4. underextension
5. coining

SAMPLE TEST QUESTIONS

1. d	11. c
2. d	12. a
3. b	13. c
4. b	14. b
5. d	15. d
6. b	16. c
7. a	17. b
8. d	18. c
9. a	19. a
10. b	20. d

Chapter 12
Early Social and Emotional Development

OUTLINE

Use this outline as you read the chapter. Enter your questions, comments, and notes in the space provided. Write down terms or statements you don't understand, with their page numbers.

THEORIES OF EARLY SOCIAL DEVELOPMENT
Learning Objective 12.1: Understand the major theoretical approaches to early social development.

Evolutionary and Biological Approaches

Environmental/Learning Approaches

Cognitive-Developmental Approaches

Sociocultural Approaches

MUTUAL REGULATION BETWEEN INFANTS AND CAREGIVERS
Learning Objective 12.2: Understand the development of early communication between the infant and caregiver.

Crying

Emotions and the Affective System

Focus on Research
Children's Ability to Recognize Emotions from Faces

Face-to-Face Interactions

TEMPERAMENT
Learning Objective 12.3: Define temperament and describe its role in child development

Defining Temperament

Conceptualizing Temperament

Temperament and Social Interactions

Temperament and Behaviour Problems

ATTACHMENT
Learning Objective 12.4: Explain the role of attachment in child development.

Developmental Course of Attachment

Assessing Attachment

Canadian Contributions
Mary Ainsworth

Determinants of Attachment

Research Classic
Mother Love: Harlow's Studies of Attachment

Consequences of Attachment

EFFECTS OF EARLY EXPERIENCE
Learning Objective 12.5 Explain how early experience can affect later social, emotional, and cognitive development.

Effects of Early Daycare

Application
Fostering Positive Teacher-Child Relationships during Early Childhood

Early Childhood Education and Care in Canada

Effects of Trauma

Effects of Abuse

Effects of Childhood Hospitalization

Short-Answer Questions

Upon completion of Chapter 12 you should be able to discuss the following topics. Check off those you are confident that you can discuss well. Re-read the material in the text for the topics about which you are less confident. Record the important points from your reading in the space below each topic.

1.   Outline the major arguments of each of the following four major theoretical approaches to attachment:

       evolutionary and biological

       environmental/learning

       cognitive-developmental

       sociocultural

2.   Briefly describe two conditions necessary for us to conclude that crying serves as a form of communication.

3.   Briefly describe the development and expression of emotions in infancy, and discuss the role of the social environment in emotional development.

4.   Describe the development of children's ability to recognize emotions.

5.   Briefly describe the importance of newborn cycles to mother-infant interaction.

6.   Discuss the consequences of disruption in infant-mother interactions.

7.   Explain why premature infants may be at greater risk for being abused than are full-term babies, with reference to mother-infant interaction.

8.   Present three important questions that have guided attempts to define temperament.

9.   Describe the major characteristics of the following three behavioural styles identified by Thomas and Chess of the New York Longitudinal Project:

       the *easy* baby

       the *difficult* baby

       the *slow-to-warm-up* baby

10.   Identify and describe the major characteristics of the dimensions of temperament comprising the EAS model.

11.   Discuss the two areas of individual temperamental differences described by Rothbart.

12.   Briefly discuss three explanations for the finding that *difficult* babies display more behaviour problems in early childhood.

13.   Explain what is meant by the term *inhibition* and discuss the relevance of this characteristic to shyness in children.

14.   Outline and describe the three phases of the development of attachment.

15.   Briefly outline the key components of the Strange Situation procedure.

16.   Describe the Strange-Situation behaviour of infants displaying each of the four patterns of attachment.

17.   Describe the AQS method for assessing attachment.

18.   Discuss how patterns of attachment may be related to culture.

19.   Briefly discuss how maternal responsiveness and infant temperament are related to attachment.

20.   Describe the four attachment styles underlying mothers' descriptions of their own childhood attachment relations using the Adult Attachment Interview.

21.   Describe the cognitive and social consequences of secure and insecure attachment.

22.   Discuss the findings of studies examining the effects of early daycare and attachment.

23.   Describe the characteristics of *post-traumatic stress disorder* (PTSD) in children. What types of situations are most often associated with PTSD?

24.   Briefly discuss how infant abuse and neglect and attachment are related.

KEY TERMS

Upon completion of Chapter 12, you should be able to define the following terms.

Primary caregiver   _____

_____

Socialization   _____

_____

Social cognition _____

_____

Internal working models _____

_____

Emotions   _____

_____

Affect _____

_____

Display rules _____

_____

Microanalysis _____

_____

Interactional synchrony _____

_____

Affect mirroring _____

_____

Temperament _____

_____

Goodness of fit _____

_____

New York Longitudinal Study (NYLS) _____

_____

EAS model _____

_____

Inhibition _____

_____

Maternal bonding _____

_____

Wariness of strangers   _____

_____

Separation protest   _____

_____

Strange situation procedure   _____

_____

Attachment Q-Set (AQS)   _____

_____

Adult attachment interview   _____

_____

FILL-IN EXERCISES

Fill in the word or words that best fit in the spaces below.

1.   The term _____ refers to the process through which society molds the child's beliefs, expectations, and behaviour.

2.   Children's and adults' knowledge of human behaviour and social interactions is referred to as _____ _____.

3.   Some theorists believe that infants and caregivers develop *internal* _____ _____ of each other that they then use to interpret events and predict how others will behave toward them.

4.   Smiling reflecting pleasure appears in response to the human voice or a moving face at around _____ or _____ weeks of age.

5.   _____ _____ are the expectations and attitudes a society holds toward the expression of affect.

6.   When the mother comes to recognize the baby's cycles of attention and inattention, and adjusts her behaviour to these cycles, mother and baby develop an *interactional* _____ in behaviour.

7.   *Affect _____* refers to the degree to which caregivers gauge their communicative behaviours to respond to input from their infants.

8.   The New York Longitudinal Study identified three early behavioural styles: the _____ baby, the _____, baby, and the _____ baby.

9.   According to the EAS model, temperament can be measured along three dimensions. _____ refers to how quickly the baby becomes aroused; _____ describes the baby's tempo; and _____ refers to the baby's preference for being with other people. A fourth component, _____, refers to the child's response to unfamiliar people.

10.   Rothbart views temperament as consisting of individual differences in two areas: _____ and _____.

11.   Jerome Kagan's research reveals that children who are quick to respond negatively to an unfamiliar situation may be displaying a temperamental trait called _____.

12.   Some researchers believe that skin-to-skin contact during a sensitive period immediately after birth is important for the development of maternal _____.

13.   Three general phases of attachment can be described. In Phase 1, infants display _____ social responsiveness. In Phase 2, they display _____ social responsiveness. In Phase 3, they display _____ attachment.

14.   Mary Ainsworth classified mother-infant attachment into three categories. Pattern B infants are considered _____ attached; pattern A infants are called insecure- _____; pattern C infants are called insecure- _____. More decently, a fourth category, pattern D, labelled insecure _____, has been identified.

15.   Harlow's research demonstrated that the most significant factor in attachment is not the opportunity for feeding, but the opportunity to cling and snuggle, a phenomenon he called _____ comfort.

16.   Researchers using the Adult Attachment Interview report the following: _____ mothers claim to have difficulty recalling and appear to assign little significance to their childhood; _____ mothers tend to dwell on their early experiences; _____ mothers have experienced attachment-related trauma that they have not yet dealt with, and _____ mothers present an objective and balanced picture of their childhood.

17.   _____ _____ _____ is a disorder in which a particularly stressful event results in later emotional symptoms, including re-experiencing the event, increased responsiveness to the outside world, a tendency to be easily startled, and nightmares.

18.   Parental maltreatment (overstimulation and understimulation) seems related to attachment: _____ has been linked to insecure-resistant attachment (pattern C), while _____ has been linked to the insecure-avoidant (pattern A) pattern of attachment.

APPLICATION

Freud felt that the mother-infant relationship is the first love relationship experienced by an individual, and that the attachment relationship forms the basis for all later love relations experienced by the infant. Other theorists also believe that secure or insecure attachment in infancy may set the stage for secure or insecure romantic relationships in adulthood.

1.   Does the notion that attachment in infancy may affect later love relations make sense to you?

2.   How could you go about researching this possible relationship? What type of design would you use?

3.   Suppose you do, indeed, find that people who developed an insecure attachment with their caregivers in infancy have difficulty forming close relationships with others as adults. Is it necessarily true that the difficulties they have with their adult relationships are **because** of their insecure attachment in infancy? Can you think of any other possible explanation (e.g., the role of temperament)?

USING WHAT YOU HAVE LEARNED

In Chapter 12, you read about the importance of caregiver–infant attachment, and about characteristics of caregivers that can either foster or hinder development of a secure attachment. You also read about the controversy over working mothers and infant daycare. Suppose that a friend of yours is a new mother. She wants to return to work, but is agonizing over the decision to place her infant in daycare. She is particularly concerned with choosing the "right" daycare.

1.   What would you advise her to look for in a daycare?

2.   What characteristics in the daycare providers should she look for?

3.   She worries the baby will become attached to the daycare provider rather than her. Is she right? Will the baby become attached to the daycare provider? Would that mean the baby cannot develop a secure attachment to her mother?

SAMPLE TEST QUESTIONS

1. The notion that the process of natural selection has provided infants and mothers with innate behaviours designed to ensure the infant's survival is attributable to:

    a. Jerome Kagan
    b. John Bowlby
    c. Mary Rothbart
    d. Robert Plomin

2. Which of the following is characteristic of the ethological approach to early social development?

    a. Babies develop internal working models of their caregivers and themselves that they use to interpret events.
    b. When they encounter an unfamiliar person or situation, babies respond with uncertainty to the discrepancy between the situation and their representations of how things typically are.
    c. Mother-infant social behaviours result from interaction between the two individuals, with each influencing the behaviour of the other.
    d. The mother's job is to "read" the infant's signals and decide what is wrong, what she should do, and when it is effective.

3. According to environmental/learning approaches, how should an infant respond if his mother does not respond to his smiling and vocalizations?

    a. He will develop an internal working model of his mother as unresponsive, which will interfere with the development of attachment.
    b. He will perceive this reaction as discrepant from his cognitive representation for his mother's typical behaviour, and will react with uncertainty.
    c. He will decrease, or perhaps stop, his smiling and vocalization.
    d. He will try to motivate the mother to provide adequate caregiving by crying.

4. Smiling to indicate pleasure first appears:

    a. immediately after birth
    b. during the first week
    c. after 10 to 12 weeks
    d. after 5 or 6 months

5. Jeffrey got his finger caught in the door. Although it wasn't seriously injured, it really hurt. He tried hard to hold back the tears, because he knows that "big boys don't cry." His attempt not to cry shows his understanding of his culture's

    a. level of affect mirroring
    b. emotional display rules
    c. internal working models
    d. expectations about social referencing

6.   Social referencing refers to:

   a.   the way in which the mother comes to recognize and adjust her behaviour with reference to the infant's cycles of attention and inattention
   b.   the process of comparing a social situation to a schema that the infant has developed for similar situations
   c.   the expectations an infant develops with reference to her caregiver's social behaviour
   d.   the infant's use of cues from her caregivers to determine how to react when she encounters an unfamiliar object or person

7.   Which of the following is **NOT** one of the three behavioural styles identified by Thomas and Chess?

   a.   the difficult baby
   b.   the hard-to-slow-down baby
   c.   the slow-to-warm-up baby
   d.   the easy baby

8.   Little Mazen's eating and feeding schedules are not very predictable. He cries often, seldom seems to be in a good mood, and reacts intensely to changes in his environment. Which of Thomas and Chess's behavioural styles would best describe Mazen?

   a.   the difficult baby
   b.   the hard-to-slow-down baby
   c.   the slow-to-warm-up baby
   d.   the easy baby

9.   Of babies that can be classified according to the Thomas and Chess typology, the smallest percentage are described as:

   a.   easy
   b.   slow-to-warm-up
   c.   hard-to-slow-down
   d.   difficult

10.   The "A" in Plomin's EAS model of temperament refers to:

   a.   the infant's preference for being with other people
   b.   how quickly a baby becomes aroused by and responds negatively to stimulation from the environment
   c.   the baby's tempo and energy use
   d.   the adaptability of the baby to changing situations

11.   Rothbart's "Reactivity" is similar to Plomin's dimension of:

   a.   Emotionality   b.   Activity
   c.   Sociability   d.   Melancholy

12.   Kagan and his colleagues describe a temperamental response style, called _____, in which infants react to unfamiliar people and situations with timidity, shyness, and fearfulness.

   a.   sociability
   b.   inhibition
   c.   insecure-avoidant
   d.   emotional reactivity

13.   Some researchers believe that maternal bonding takes place during a sensitive period occurring

   a.   immediately after birth
   b.   throughout the first two months of life
   c.   across the first year of life
   d.   across the first two years of life

14.   Behaviours indicating that the infant has formed an attachment with her primary caregiver can be observed:

   a.   in the first few hours after birth
   b.   during the first two months of life
   c.   at around 3 months of age
   d.   at around 8 months of age

15.   Mary Ainsworth's typology of attachment consists of all of the following, except:

   a.   insecure-inhibited
   b.   insecure-avoidant
   c.   securely-attached
   d.   insecure-resistant

16.   Babies who react to the Strange Situation with distress when the mother leaves, but respond enthusiastically when she returns, are classified as:

   a.   insecure-inhibited
   b.   insecure-avoidant
   c.   securely-attached
   d.   insecure-resistant

17.   When exposed to the Strange Situation, little Marion was distressed, even when her mother was there. She was especially upset when her mother left. When her mother returned, although Marion was relieved, she also seemed angry with her mother. Marion's attachment would be classified as:

   a.   insecure-inhibited
   b.   insecure-resistant
   c.   insecure-avoidant
   d.   securely-attached

18.   Which of the following is unlikely to be associated with secure attachment?

    a.   delaying responding to the infants' crying in order to not "spoil" the baby
    b.   feeding the baby at a comfortable pace
    c.   affectionate and tender handling of the infant
    d.   actually, all of the above are associated with secure attachment

19.   In response to the Adult Attachment Interview, *unresolved* mothers

    a.   claim to have difficulty recalling their childhoods, appearing to assign little significance to them
    b.   tend to dwell on early experiences that they describe in a confused and emotional manner
    c.   have experienced attachment-related trauma that they have not yet dealt with
    d.   none of the above

20.   Studies have found that, in comparison to Pattern A or C infants, Pattern B infants tend later to be:

    a.   better problem solvers
    b.   more socially competent
    c.   less likely to develop emotional or behaviour problems
    d.   all of the above

ANSWERS

FILL-IN EXERCISES

1. socialization   2. social cognition   3. working models   4. ten, twelve   5. display rules   6. synchrony
7. mirroring   8. easy, difficult, slow-to-warm-up   9. emotionality; activity; sociability; shyness
10. reactivity; self-regulation   11. inhibition   12. bonding   13. indiscriminate; discriminate; focused
14. securely; avoidant; resistant; disorganized/disoriented   15. contact   16. dismissing; preoccupied; unresolved; autonomous   17. posttraumatic stress disorder   18. understimulation; overstimulation

USING WHAT YOU HAVE LEARNED

1. Look for a daycare that provides a high level of care and where the caregivers are regular and consistent individuals who are involved with the children.

2. The same sorts of reliable and affectionate care that promote parent-infant attachment should be important characteristics of the daycare providers.

3. If the daycare provider provides high quality care, the infant may indeed become attached to her or him. This does not mean the infant will not become attached to his or her mother—infants can be attached to a small number of special people in their lives and so could be attached to mom, dad, and also their daycare provider.

SAMPLE TEST QUESTIONS

1. b   11. a
2. d   12. b
3. c   13. a
4. c   14. d
5. b   15. a
6. d   16. c
7. b   17. b
8. a   18. a
9. d   19. c
10. c   20. d

Chapter 13
Development of the Self

OUTLINE

Use this outline as you read the chapter. Enter your questions, comments, and notes in the space provided. Write down terms or statements you don't understand, with their page numbers.

THEORIES OF THE SELF

Learning Objective 13.1: Compare and contrast five theoretical perspectives on the development of the self-system.

Cognitive-Developmental Approaches

Environmental/Learning Approaches

Evolutionary and Biological Approaches

Research Classic
Monkey in the Mirror: Primate Self-Recognition

Sociocultural Approaches

SELF-KNOWLEDGE

Learning Objective 13.2: Trace the development of self-knowledge from infancy, identifying the processes by which changes in the self-system occur.

Discovery of the Self in Infancy

Self-Recognition

Developmental Changes in Self-Descriptions

Focus on Research
Self-Continuity, Cultural Identity, and Suicide in First Nations Youth

SELF-EVALUATION

Learning Objective 13.3: Describe the development of self-esteem, ways to measure it, and the contexts that shape the way children evaluate themselves.

Measuring Self-Esteem

The Developmental Progression of Self-Esteem

Gender Differences in Self-Esteem

Academic Self-Concept

Application
Possible Selves and Academic Achievement

SELF-REGULATION

Learning Objective 13.4: Analyze the mechanisms and processes by which children develop self-control.

The Emergence of Self-Control

Compliance

Resistance to Temptation

Delay of Gratification

SHORT-ANSWER QUESTIONS

Upon completion of Chapter 13 you should be able to discuss the following topics. Check off those you are confident that you can discuss well. Re-read the material in the text for the topics about which you are less confident. Record the important points from your reading in the space below each topic.

1.   Explain what is meant by each of the following components of the self-system: *self-knowledge*, *self-evaluation*, and *self-regulation.*

2.   Describe how self-schemas influence the way children understand and relate to the world around them.

3.   Outline the five stages of Selman's model of children's progression in self-awareness.

4.   Discuss how Bandura explained the development of self-evaluation and of self-regulation in children.

5.   Describe how infant-caregiver interactions lead to the development of a sense of self, according to Bowlby's theory.

6.   List three questions about the self that have interested evolutionary psychologists.

7.   Explain how cultural practices influence the shaping of the self.

8.   Discuss the processes involved in the infant's development of an initial sense of separateness and of personal agency in his or her world.

9.   Describe how researchers use visual self-recognition to infer the development of self-knowledge in infants.

10.   Discuss how temperamental and attachment differences may affect self-recognition in infants.

11.   Explain the connection between *synchronic imitation* in children's play and children's self-awareness.

12.   Contrast children's self-descriptions at three Piagetian stages of cognitive development.

13.   Outline three phases of cultural identity development in ethnic minority youth.

14.   Discuss how *cultural continuity* can play a protective role in First Nations youth.

15. Briefly describe the procedures developed by Harter and by Marsh for assessing self-esteem in children.

16. Describe three factors that may account for a decrease in self-esteem as children approach adolescence.

17. Describe how boys and girls differ in self-esteem.

18. Discuss age and gender differences in academic self-concept.

19. Contrast children who display a *mastery-oriented* pattern differ with those who display a *helpless* pattern.

20. Contrast the beliefs of children who hold an *entity model* with those who hold an *incremental model* of intelligence. How are these views related to the mastery-oriented and helpless patterns?

21. Discuss how praise and criticism can affect children's academic self-concept.

22. Explain how children's social comparisons may affect their self-evaluations of competence, and how such comparisons change across grade level.

23.   Discuss three venues through which parents can positively influence their children's academic self-concept.

24.   Describe children's progression from external control to self-control.

25.   Contrast *committed compliance* with *situational compliance*.

26.   Explain how researchers assess children's resistance to temptation and discuss the factors that influence children's behaviour in such situations.

.

27.   Describe the delay-of-gratification technique. Discuss the factors that have been found to affect children's ability to delay gratification.

KEY TERMS

Upon completion of Chapter 13, you should be able to define the following terms.

Existential self _____

_____

Categorical self _____

_____

Self-system _____

_____

Self-knowledge (self-awareness) _____

_____

Self-evaluation _____

_____

Self-regulation _____

_____

Self-schema _____

_____

Self-efficacy _____

_____

Evaluative self-reactions _____

_____

Personal agency _____

_____

Visual self-recognition _____

_____

False self behaviour _____

_____

Self-esteem (self-worth) _____

_____

Looking-glass self _____

_____

Competence _____

_____

Self-consciousness _____

_____

Academic self-concept _____

_____

Entity model _____

_____

Incremental model _____

_____

Social comparison _____

_____

Possible selves _____

_____

Compliance   _____

_____

Committed compliance   _____

_____

Situational compliance   _____

_____

Forbidden toy technique _____

_____

Delay of gratification technique   _____

_____

FILL-IN EXERCISES

Fill in the word or words that best fit in the spaces below.

1. The "I," or _____ self is the subjective experience of the world whereas the "Me," or _____ self is an objective entity seen and evaluated in the world.

2. Self-_____ is the part of the self-system concerned with what children know about themselves. Self-_____ is the part of the self-system concerned with children's opinions of themselves and their abilities. Self-_____ is the part of the self-system that is concerned with self-control.

3. Selman's model is most concerned with children's self-_____.

4. Self-_____ are constructed over time and serve primarily to organize self-related information.

5. An individual's view of his/her own ability to carry out various behaviours is referred to by Bandura as the person's self-_____.

6. Evaluative self-_____ is Bandura's term for consequences people apply to themselves as a result of meeting or failing to meet their personal standards.

7. Along with infants' knowledge that they exist apart from the things around them comes an understanding of personal _____; that is, an understanding that they can be the causes of events in their world.

8.   _____ _____ describes the play of two preverbal children with similar toys in a similar fashion, involving coordinated action. This type of play involves some degree of self- and other-awareness.

9.   As babies approach age 2, many display an increasing awareness of self through their use of pronouns such as _____ and _____.

10.   Babies do not recognize their image in a mirror before about _____ months, and self-recognition does not occur reliably until about _____ months.

11.   By _____ years of age, many children display knowledge of some of their most basic characteristics, such as whether they are girls or boys, and that they are children rather than adults.

12.   Adolescents can display _____ behaviour, meaning that, when necessary, they can behave in ways that do not reflect their true selves.

13.   According to the idea of the _____ self, the psychological portraits we paint of ourselves are based on how we think others see us.

14.   Many investigators report that at about age 11 or 12, children's self-_____ tends frequently to decrease, only to increase again over the subsequent years.

15.   Typically, children's academic self-concept is highest in _____, but declines across the next four grades.

16.   According to Dweck's model, _____-oriented children view failure experiences as an opportunity to learn from their experiences, whereas _____ children avoid future challenges, because they view failure as a sign of low self-worth.

17.   In terms of their theories of intelligence, some children believe in a(n) _____ model, in which the amount of a person's intelligence is fixed and unchangeable, whereas others believe in a(n) _____ model, in which a person's intelligence can grow with experience and learning.

18.   Children with _____ *(lower/ higher)* opinions of their academic competence tend also to make fewer social comparisons.

19.   _____ *(fathers/mothers)* of children with high academic self-concept have been found to be warmer and more supportive in their interactions than those of children with low academic self-concept.

20.   _____ selves is the term used to refer to concepts of the self in the future that represent one's goals, dreams, hopes, and fears.

21.   _____ compliance results when the child embraces the caregiver's agenda and adopts it as his or her own.

Application

Situation

Each Friday afternoon, the children at Northumberland Nursery School celebrate the weekend by having cookies and juice with their teachers and caregivers at the end of the day. When the cookies are brought out, the children quickly gather around, eager to help themselves, but must wait until their teacher tells them it's cookie time. Compare this situation to what you read in the sections on compliance, resistance to temptation, and the forbidden toy technique.

Questions to answer

1.   What strategies would you advise to help the children resist the temptation to dive into the cookies before it is cookie time?

2.   Would your advice be different if the children were 6- or 7-years old compared to 3- or 4-years old?

3.   Is there anything the parents and teachers should not do?

4.   Is there any advantage to teaching the children to delay helping themselves to the cookies?

USING WHAT YOU HAVE LEARNED

Following graduation, you get a job working as a psychological consultant with the local school. The school is concerned that there seem to be some children who aren't able to deal well with negative feedback concerning their school performance. Often when they encounter failure, they don't believe they "have what it takes" to do well at school. The school principal asks for your help. Based on what you've read in Chapter 13 concerning academic self-concept, especially Dweck's motivational model of achievement, how would you address these questions?

1.   Do children really react differently to the same experiences, so that some cope well with failure and keep trying, while others give up?

2.   What factors might cause such differences between types of children?

3.   Could it have to do with how children are treated in the classroom? Is there anything teachers could do to help the children who don't cope well?

4.   Is this really important anyway? Will children just grow out of this, or should we be concerned?

SAMPLE TEST QUESTIONS

1. Children's opinions of themselves and their abilities are referred to as:

    a.   self-knowledge
    b.   self-evaluation
    c.   self-centeredness
    d.   egocentrism

2. The part of the self-system that would be concerned with children's ability to resist temptation is:

    a.   self-knowledge
    b.   self evaluation
    c.   self-regulation
    d.   self-centeredness

3. The notion of self-schemas is attributable to which approach?

    a.   Piaget's theory
    b.   Selman's model
    c.   Information-Processing model
    d.   Self-Efficacy theory

4. According to Selman's research, believing that the self cannot ever be completely known characterizes which period of development?

    a.   early childhood
    b.   middle childhood
    c.   preadolescence
    d.   adolescence

5. The belief that inner thoughts and feelings are directly represented in outward appearance or behaviour characterizes which level of Selman's model of children's awareness of the self?

    a.   level 0
    b.   level 1
    c.   level 2
    d.   level 3

6. Children who are high in self-esteem and who are not depressed are more likely to recall:

    a.   negative personal traits
    b.   positive personal traits
    c.   about equal proportions of positive and negative personal traits
    d.   it would be impossible to predict how they would recall the traits

7.   The notion of self-efficacy is associated with which theorist?

    a.   Bandura
    b.   Dweck
    c.   Harter
    d.   Selman

8.   In contrast to Caucasian American children, Japanese children

    a.   are taught to sacrifice their personal interest for the sake of interpersonal harmony
    b.   are taught to defend their individual rights and to respect the rights of others
    c.   are taught that they have the right to an opinion very early in life
    d.   are socialized for independence from an early age

9.   In one study, babies aged 6 months and older watched an adult model eat a Cheerio. They were then given a Cheerio and instructed either to feed it to themselves or feed it to their mothers. Results indicated that

    a.   more infants fed the Cheerio to their mothers than to themselves
    b.   infants were equally inclined to feed the Cheerio to themselves or to their mothers
    c.   most infants simply played with the Cheerio rather than feeding themselves or their mothers
    d.   more infants fed the Cheerio to themselves than to their mothers

10.   An infant looking in a mirror notices a red mark on her forehead in the reflection and touches her forehead. This behaviour does not occur until at least _____ of age.

    a.   8 months
    b.   12 months
    c.   15 months
    d.   24 months

11.   Synchronic imitation in the play of preverbal children shows evidence of:

    a.   other awareness
    b.   self-knowledge
    c.   self-recognition
    d.   self- and other-regulation

12.   When asked to describe himself, Daniel replies: "I love guitar, and I'm really an easy-going kind of guy." Based on research into children's self-descriptions, we may conclude that Daniel is likely:

    a.   3-years old
    b.   5-years old
    c.   8-years old
    d.   13-years old

13.   When asked what kind of person she is, Francine replies: "I have very long hair and I live in a white house." Francine's self-description indicates that she is likely at what Piagetian stage of development?

    a.   sensorimotor
    b.   preoperational
    c.   concrete operational
    d.   formal operational

14.   Eleven-year old Suzie has begun to question her abilities, her appearance, and so on, although she used to be a fairly optimistic, confident little girl. Her parents have noticed the change, and are concerned. What would you tell them?

    a.   This is a serious change, and likely signals even further problems to come as she enters high school.
    b.   This is a serious problem, and likely has been with her since kindergarten; her parents were likely mistaken when they assumed she had been self-confident earlier on.
    c.   Her parents are likely wrong; it is very unlikely for self-esteem to be an issue before adolescence.
    d.   This is a fairly common occurrence; it may not be a major cause for concern since many children's esteem increases again during the high school years.

15.   Which of the following is LEAST likely to be related to decreasing self-esteem as children approach adolescence?

    a.   remaining in the same school
    b.   biological changes associated with puberty
    c.   increasing self-consciousness
    d.   ALL of the above are EQUALLY associated with drops in self-esteem

16.   According to Dweck's model, children who display the helpless pattern generally believe that:

    a.   their lack of success is the result of a lack of ability
    b.   effort is more important to success than ability
    c.   their lack of success comes from lack of ability, but that ability can grow through experience
    d.   all of the above

17.   In terms of the emergence of self-control, most children begin to pay attention to simple standards set by others or by themselves, and monitor their activities with respect to those standards during the _____ year of age.

    a.   first
    b.   second
    c.   third
    d.   fourth

18.   Which of the following is likely to influence children's behaviour in the forbidden-toy procedure?

     a.   Teaching children to develop their own plans or strategies for dealing with the temptation to play with the toy.
     b.   Providing children with a good rationale for the prohibition against playing with the toy.
     c.   Seeing an adult break the rule and play with the toy.
     d.   All of the above

19.   Which of the following is true concerning delay of gratification?

     a.   Ability to delay of gratification is not a very stable characteristic, fluctuating wildly from childhood to adolescence.
     b.   Ability to delay gratification seems related to children's social competence.
     c.   Preschoolers display an impressive understanding of delay-of-gratification strategies, even at such a young age.
     d.   all of the above

20.   The ability to delay gratification in the preschool years is predictive of children's functioning 10 years later in which of the following areas?

     a.   self-knowledge
     b.   creativity
     c.   coping with stress
     d.   artistic appreciation

ANSWERS

FILL-IN EXERCISES

1. existential, categorical   2. knowledge (awareness); evaluation; regulation   3. awareness (or knowledge)
4. schemas   5. efficacy   6. reactions   7. agency   8. synchronic imitation   9. me, mine   10. 15; 24
11. two   12. false-self   13. looking-glass   14. esteem   15. kindergarten   16. mastery; helpless
17. entity; incremental   18. lower   19. fathers   20. possible   21. committed

APPLICATION

1. Use self-instructions to help resist temptation; provide a good rationale for not taking the cookies; keep the cookies out of sight until later.
2. With older children, self-instructions that are relevant to the task (e.g., "I must not take a cookie") are most effective, whereas with younger children, any self-instruction seems to work.
3. Yes. Seeing an adult break the rule reduces children's resistance to temptation. If the adults take a cookie early, the children likely will too.
4.. Yes. Learning to delay gratification is associated with later academic success, getting along with peers, coping with problems, and confidence and self-reliance.

USING WHAT YOU HAVE LEARNED

1. Yes. Some children display a mastery-oriented pattern whereas others display a helpless pattern.
2. Feelings of self-worth seem to underlie such differences. Attitudes, expectations, and behaviours of parents are also important, as are children's implicit theories of intelligence.
3. Yes. Criticism and person-oriented praise can serve to increase vulnerability to failure. Feedback directed at children's strategies is most effective.
4. It is important. Academic self-concept actually influences later academic achievement.

SAMPLE TEST QUESTIONS

1. b	11. a
2. c	12. d
3. c	13. b
4. d	14. d
5. b	15. a
6. b	16. a
7. a	17. c
8. a	18. d
9. d	19. b
10. c	20. c

Chapter 14
Moral Development

OUTLINE

Use this outline as you read the chapter. Enter your questions, comments, and notes in the space provided. Write down terms or statements you don't understand, with their page numbers.

THEORIES OF MORAL DEVELOPMENT
Learning Objective 14.1: Understand four theoretical approaches to the study of moral development.

Cognitive-Developmental Approaches

Evolutionary and Biological Approaches

Environmental/Learning Approaches

Sociocultural Approaches

MORAL REASONING
Learning Objective 14.2: Understand what research has found concerning children's moral reasoning.

Evaluating Piaget's Model

Evaluating Kohlberg's Model

Evaluating Turiel's Model

Distributive Justice and Retributive Justice

Social and Family Influences on Moral Reasoning

On the Cutting Edge
Children's Reasoning about the Morality of Peer Exclusion

Moral Reasoning and Moral Conduct

PROSOCIAL BEHAVIOUR

Learning Objective 14.3: Understand the development of prosocial behaviour and identify its determinants.

Empathy and Sympathy

Development of Prosocial Behaviour

Biological Determinants of Prosocial Behaviour

Cognitive and Affective Determinants of Prosocial Behaviour

Sociocultural and Family Determinants of Prosocial Behaviour

AGGRESSION
Learning Objective 14.4: Describe the factors that contribute to aggressive behaviour, and discuss ways of reducing aggression in children.

Defining Aggression

Age and Gender Differences in Aggression

Biological Determinants of Aggression

Sociocultural and Environmental Determinants of Aggression

Cognitive and Affective Influences on Aggression

Focus on Research
Bullying and Victimization in School

Controlling Aggression

SHORT-ANSWER QUESTIONS

Upon completion of Chapter 14 you should be able to discuss the following topics. Check off those you are confident that you can discuss well. Re-read the material in the text for the topics about which you are less confident. Record the important points from your reading in the space below each topic.

1.   Outline and describe Piaget's four stages of moral reasoning.

2.   Explain how interactions with peers influence moral development, according to Piaget's theory.

3.   Describe Kohlberg's cognitive theory of moral development, outlining the three levels of moral reasoning and the two stages comprising each level.

4.   Discuss how Turiel's model explains moral reasoning.

5.   Present the evolutionary/biological position regarding altruistic and aggressive behaviour.

6.   Explain how social learning theory views moral development.

7.   Discuss how sociocultural approaches view moral development.

8.   Describe how research has supported Piaget's theory of moral development. What aspects of the theory have not held up well to empirical scrutiny?

9.   Discuss the aspects of Kohlberg's theory that have been supported and those that have not been supported by empirical research.

10.   Discuss the findings of research evaluating the claims of Turiel's model of moral reasoning.

11.   Explain how children reason concerning distributive and retributive justice.

12.   Briefly describe how peers and parents influence moral reasoning.

13.   Distinguish between each of the following classes of parental discipline: power assertion, love withdrawal, and induction. How are these classes of discipline related to moral internalization?

14.   Briefly explain how Piaget, Kohlberg, and social-learning theorists view the relationship between moral reasoning and moral conduct.

15.   Outline Hoffman's five stages in the development of empathy.

16.   Discuss the findings of research examining helping and sharing in young children.

17.   Distinguish between the following three methods of conflict resolution in children: negotiation, disengagement, and coercion. How does the use of these strategies change with age?

18.   Discuss how age and culture may be important considerations in children's peacemaking.

19.   Explain how genetic factors might produce differences in prosocial behaviour.

20.   Briefly discuss how empathy, prosocial reasoning, and mental state understanding contribute to children's prosocial behaviour.

21.   Describe how parents can influence children's prosocial behaviour.

22.   Distinguish between hostile aggression, instrumental aggression, and relational aggression.

23.   Explain how each of the following three mechanisms may indicate a biological basis for aggression:

hormones

genes

temperament

24.   Describe how the expression of aggression changes across age.

25.   Explain the differences in aggression displayed by boys and by girls.

26.   Describe how family processes, such as modelling and coercive interactions, may encourage aggressive behaviour in children.

27.   Argue against the notion that all aggressive children have no friends.

28.   Discuss the roles that peers play in bullying.

29.   Describe the four goals of the Olweus anti-bullying program.

30.   Discuss what researchers have found concerning children's exposure to violence on television, in video games, and in real life.

31.   Explain the social-cognitive differences that have been found between aggressive and non-aggressive children.

32.   Describe several successful techniques for reducing aggression in children.

KEY TERMS

Upon completion of Chapter 14, you should be able to define the following terms.

Moral dilemmas _____

_____

Moral realism _____

_____

Immanent justice _____

_____

Moral relativism _____

_____

Preconventional level _____

_____

Conventional level _____

_____

Postconventional level _____

_____

Social conventions _____

_____

Paradox of altruism _____

_____

Kin selection _____

_____

Reciprocal altruism _____

_____

Dominance hierarchy _____

_____

Prosocial behaviour _____

_____

Empathy _____

_____

Sympathy _____

_____

Peacemaking _____

_____

Aggression _____

_____

Hostile (retaliatory) aggression _____

_____

Instrumental aggression _____

_____

Relational aggression _____

_____

Coercive family process _____

_____

Displaced aggression _____

_____

Catharsis _____

_____

FILL-IN EXERCISES

Fill in the word or words that best fit in the spaces below.

1.   Investigations that focus on children's behaviour in moral situations examine moral _____, whereas those looking at how children think about their behaviour examine moral _____.

2.   Piaget examined children playing games such as marbles because of his interest in how they created and enforced _____.

3.   Young children's notion that punishment must always occur when a rule is broken was described by Piaget as _____ _____.

4.   Considering motives and intentions to be as important as the outcomes of behaviour characterizes Piaget's stage of _____ _____.

5.   From his research, Kohlberg concluded that moral reasoning develops in three predictable levels which he termed _____, _____, and _____, each of which contains _____ stages.

6.   Kohlberg's model shares several characteristics with that of Piaget. Each stage forms a structured _____, with children in that stage generally responding consistently to different dilemmas and situations. The stages follow a(n) _____ sequence, so that children experience them all in the same order, with no regression to previous stages. Finally, the pattern of progression is _____ for all people and all cultures.

7.   Turiel believes that children's moral reasoning involves three distinct domains. The _____ domain is concerned with people's rights and welfare. The _____ domain involves social conventions. Finally, there are matters of personal choice, in which individual preferences take priority.

8.   Behaviours that benefit someone else but offer no obvious benefit to the individual performing them are _____ behaviours.

9.   The notion of _____ selection proposes that humans behave in ways that increase the chances for the survival and reproduction of their genes rather than of themselves.

10.   _____ altruism is a process that suggests that people are programmed to be helpful because: (1) it increases the likelihood that some day they will in turn receive aid from the person they helped, or (2) by helping someone else in their social group they ensure the survival of genes similar to their own.

11.   A _____ _____ refers to a structured social group in which members higher on the power ladder control those who are lower, through aggression and threats.

12.   Cross-cultural studies of Kohlberg's theory find that in many nontechnical societies, individuals rarely progress to the _____ stage.

13.   The issue of how to distribute a limited amount of resources among a group of deserving people is referred to as _____ _____.

14.   Use of commands, threats, and physical force is a disciplinary practice referred to as _____ _____; the use of verbal disapproval, ridicule, or withholding of affection is described as _____ _____.

15. The disciplinary practice that is associated with the most advanced levels of moral reasoning in North American children is _____.

16. _____ refers to the ability to vicariously experience another's emotional state or condition, whereas _____ involves feeling concern for another in reaction to his or her situation or emotional state, without necessarily sharing the same emotions.

17. Babies crying when they hear another baby crying may be an early sign of _____.

18. Conflict can be resolved in three broad ways. _____ includes compromise and intervention by a third party, such as another peer or a teacher. _____ includes withdrawal and shifting the focus or topic. _____ occurs when one party gives in to the demands of another, sometimes in response to threats or other aggressive ploys.

19. A friendly postconflict reunion between former opponents is described as _____.

20. Name-calling, teasing, and threats are referred to as _____ aggression, whereas hitting, kicking, and biting are called _____ aggression.

21. Aggression aimed at inflicting pain or injury is called _____ aggression, whereas aggressive behaviour intended to obtain something is termed _____ aggression.

22. Beginning in the preschool years and extending into adolescence, girls are more likely to display _____ aggression than are boys.

23. There is evidence that the hormone _____ plays a role in aggression.

24. Gerald Patterson referred to the method by which some families control one another through aggression and other coercive means as _____ _____ _____.

25. Retaliatory aggression directed at a person or object other than the one against whom retaliation is desired is referred to as _____ _____.

26. _____ is a psychoanalytic belief that the likelihood of aggression can be reduced by viewing aggression or by engaging in high-energy behaviours. This belief _____ (*has/has not*) been supported by research.

USING WHAT YOU HAVE LEARNED

Children are participating in an interview designed to assess their moral reasoning, using a variation of Piaget's moral dilemmas. The interviewer presents the following situations:

> Jeffrey is called to dinner by his mother. While coming to dinner, he accidentally knocks over a tray of dishes that was behind the door to the dining room, breaking 10 cups.

James has been told not to take any cookies from the cupboard. He goes ahead anyway, and while taking a cookie, breaks a saucer.

The interviewer asks each child whether Jeffrey or James did the worse thing, and what punishment each deserves. What do the following responses indicate about the children's moral reasoning?

#1 by Maria. "Jeffrey did the worse thing because he broke more things."

#2 by Robert. "James deserves more punishment than Jeffrey. Jeffrey didn't really mean it."

APPLICATION

You have been asked to write a short pamphlet offering advice for parents on how to promote prosocial behaviour and discourage aggressive behaviour in their children. Based on what you have read in Chapter 14, what advice would you give to parents with reference to each of the following five topics?

1.   When and how to reward and punish your child.

2.   Should you be concerned about the effects of television and videogames?

3.   Talking to your child about moral issues.

4.   Teaching your child how to deal with conflict.

5.   Differences between boys and girls.

SAMPLE TEST QUESTIONS

1.   Piaget investigated children's understanding of rules by:

    a.   observing them playing marbles
    b.   presenting them with prosocial dilemmas in which the individual must decide whether to help someone, often at some personal expense
    c.   presenting them with moral dilemmas that involve choosing between obeying a rule or breaking a rule for the benefit of an individual
    d.   presenting them with rewards and asking them to divide them up equitably among their peers

2.   All of the following are characteristic of Piaget's second stage of moral development, except:

    a.   consideration of amount of damage when judging whether an act is morally wrong
    b.   consideration of an individual's intentions when judging whether an act is morally wrong
    c.   view of rules as absolute
    d.   belief that punishment must always occur if a rule is broken

3.   Piaget uses the term heteronomous to refer to:

       a.   the notion that punishment must always occur if a rule is broken
       b.   the tendency to evaluate moral situations only in terms of their objective and physical consequences
       c.   the belief that punishment must always occur if a rule is broken
       d.   the belief that morality is dictated by people in authority

4.   Children in Piaget's third stage of moral development view rules as:

       a.   unchangeable absolutes
       b.   agreements that can be changed to fit the circumstances of the moment
       c.   dictated by people in authority
       d.   applicable only to their peers (i.e., their age-mates)

5.   While driving with his father, little Billy notices a speed-limit sign. He asks his father what the sign means and his father explains that it means they shouldn't drive faster than 100 km per hour. Billy then asks his father how fast they're driving and becomes really upset to find they're driving 110 km per hour. According to Piaget's theory of moral development, Billy is likely how old?

       a.   three years   b.   five years
       c.   nine years   d.   eleven years

6.   Movement from stage to stage in Kohlberg's model closely follows the Piagetian process of:

       a.   assimilation   b.   seriation
       c.   accommodation   d.   reversibility

7.   Someone at Kohlberg's preconventional level evaluates moral dilemmas according to:

       a.   his/her own self-interests and needs   b.   the principles of fairness and justice
       c.   the concern for maintaining social order d.   the concern for social approval

8.   Social learning theorists argue that:

       a.   moral development parallels stages of cognitive development
       b.   observational learning, reinforcement, and punishment account for children's moral development
       c.   children progress through a sequence of stages of moral development that is universal
       d.   there is a strong connection between moral reasoning and moral conduct

9.   Which of the following claims of Turiel's model has been supported by recent research?

       a.   Moral reasoning involves several independent domains of social cognition.
       b.   Induction fosters moral development more than either love withdrawal or power assertion.
       c.   Young children do not consider intent when making moral judgments.
       d.   All children progress through the same stages of moral development, in the same order.

10.   Until about _____ years of age, children's distribution of rewards to others is characterized by self-interest.

a.   two   b.   four
c.   six   d.   eight

11.   By seven years of age, children use _____ as the basis for distributing rewards to others.

a.   equity
b.   reciprocity
c.   altruism
d.   empathy

12.   The form of discipline that produces the least mature forms of moral reasoning is:

a.   induction
b.   love withdrawal
c.   power assertion
d.   love assertion

13.   Martin Hoffman has proposed a five-stage model of the development of empathy. During the fourth stage:

a.   because they now can understand that others have inner states different than their own, children offer appropriate help and comfort
b.   children have difficulty distinguishing between their own and others' thoughts and feelings, and so offer help that reflects what they would like rather than what the other person needs
c.   children respond to the distress of others by comforting themselves or by seeking comfort from caregivers
d.   children reflexively cry when they hear another child crying

14.   Aggressive behaviour which is intended to obtain something is referred to as:

a.   hostile aggression
b.   displaced aggression
c.   verbal aggression
d.   instrumental aggression

15.   Which of the following is **NOT** true concerning gender differences in aggression?

a.   Boys display more aggression in preschool than do girls.
b.   In elementary school, boys become increasingly aggressive towards girls.
c.   Beginning in preschool and extending into adolescence, girls display more relational aggression than do boys.
d.   In elementary school, aggression by boys toward other boys becomes increasingly physical in nature.

16.   Studies examining the effects of televised violence report that:

a.   children imitate violent acts seen on television
b.   TV violence increases the likelihood of all other forms of aggression in children, even those that do not resemble the behaviour of the television models
c.   television violence stimulates aggression, and children who are more aggressive tend to watch even more violent television
d.   all of the above

17.   Cairns' research concerning the friendship patterns of aggressive children found:

a.   aggressive children had much fewer peer nominations of "best friend" than did nonaggressive children
b.   aggressive children were most often nominated as "best friend" by non-aggressive peers rather than by other aggressive children
c.   aggressive children tended to be largely shunned by the peer group, resulting in no peer nominations at all
d.   aggressive children had just as many peer nominations of "best friend" as did non-aggressive children

18.   Coercive family process involves:

a.   family members controlling one another through aggression and other coercive means
b.   coercing a family to deal with an aggressive child through the process of family therapy
c.   family members controlling one another through coercive means such as bribery and monetary rewards
d.   a process by which some families attempt to coerce an aggressive child to be non-aggressive through the use of rewards alone

19.   In comparison to non-aggressive children, aggressive children:

a.   show a lower level of moral reasoning
b.   show less empathy
c.   are more likely to attribute hostile motives to other children
d.   all of the above

20.   Which of the following has **NOT** proven effective in controlling aggression?

a.   catharsis
b.   parent training
c.   social-cognitive methods
d.   all of the above **HAVE** been found effective

ANSWERS

FILL-IN EXERCISES

1. conduct; reasoning   2. rules   3. immanent justice   4. moral relativism   5. preconventional; conventional; postconventional; two   6. whole; invariant; universal   7. moral; social   8. altruistic   9. kin   10. reciprocal   11. dominance hierarchy   12. fifth   13. distributive justice   14. power assertion; love withdrawal   15. induction   16. empathy; sympathy   17. empathy   18. negotiation; disengagement; coercion   19. peacemaking   20. verbal; physical   21. hostile (or retaliatory); instrumental   22. relational   23. testosterone   24. coercive family process   25.displaced aggression   26. catharsis; has not

USING WHAT YOU HAVE LEARNED

1. Maria is focusing on the amount of damage and is ignoring the good intentions of the character in the story. Such reasoning is characteristic of the stage of moral realism, Piaget's second stage.

2. Robert is focusing on the intentions of the character in the story rather than the amount of damage. This is characteristic of the stage of moral relativism, Piaget's third stage of moral reasoning.

SAMPLE TEST QUESTIONS

1. a	11. a
2. b	12. c
3. d	13. a
4. b	14. d
5. b	15. b
6. c	16. d
7. a	17. d
8. b	18. a
9. a	19. d
10. b	20. a

Chapter 15
Families and Peers

OUTLINE

Use this outline as you read the chapter. Enter your questions, comments, and notes in the space provided. Write down terms or statements you don't understand, with their page numbers.

THEORIES OF SOCIALIZATION

Learning Objective 15.1: Discuss four theoretical approaches to socialization.

Evolutionary Approaches

Environmental/Learning Approaches

Cognitive-Developmental Approaches

Sociocultural Approaches

SOCIALIZATION WITHIN THE FAMILY

Learning Objective 15.2: Analyze the influence of parents and other family members on childhood socialization.

Parenting Styles

Research Classic
Parenting Styles: The Work of Diana Baumrind

Ethnic and Cultural Factors

The Role of Fathers

The Child's Contribution

THE FAMILY AS A SYSTEM

Learning Objective 15.3: Analyze the ways that families function as a social system.

Siblings

Grandparents and Other Family Members

Divorce

Alternative Family Composition

SOCIALIZATION BY PEERS

Learning Objective 15.4 Trace the development of peer relations and discuss how peers influence each other's development.

Typical Peer Relations

Cognitive Contributions

Processes of Peer Influence

VARIATIONS IN PEER RELATIONS
Learning Objective 15.5: Discuss the contributors to and benefits of friendship.

Friendship

Popularity and Problems

Application
Interventions to Help Children with Problems

Focus on Research
Children Who are Painfully Shy and Withdrawn

FAMILY AND PEERS
Learning Objective 15.6 Understand how experiences within the family contribute to children's behaviour with friends.

Siblings and Peers

Parents and Peers

On the Cutting Edge
Peer Relations as a Source of Resilience

Short-Answer Questions

Upon completion of Chapter 15 you should be able to discuss the following topics. Check off those you are confident that you can discuss well. Re-read the material in the text for the topics about which you are less confident. Record the important points from your reading in the space below each topic.

1. Discuss the evolutionary psychologists' notion that many social behaviours, including parental caregiving and behaviours toward peers, have a biological basis.

2. Explain the social-learning perspective on how parents and peers can affect children's behaviour and development.

3. Discuss how interactions with parents and peers promote moral development and cognitive development in children according to the cognitive-developmental approach.

4. Explain how the sociocultural approach views the role of parents and peers in socialization.

5. Describe the dimensions of *parental warmth* and *parental control*.

6. Differentiate between the four styles of parenting identified by Diana Baumrind. Explain how parental warmth and parental control combine to yield these four styles.

7. Explain how ethnic and cultural factors may influence styles of parenting.

8. Compare fathers and mothers in terms of caregiving and parenting roles.

9. Explain how characteristics of the child can influence parental behaviour.

10. Describe how relationships with siblings develop with age. How do sibling relationships affect development?

11. Discuss the roles that grandparents may play in children's development.

12. Describe the short-term and longer-term effects of divorce. What factors appear to influence these effects?

13. Describe two distinct sorts of single parents who have never married.

14. Discuss the risks and benefits associated with adoption.

15. Discuss what is currently known about children of gay and lesbian parents.

16.   Describe the nature of interactions with peers in infancy.

17.   Compare and contrast two systems for classifying the play of preschoolers (i.e., according to cognitive level and according to social level).

18.   Discuss the importance and influence of the peer group in later childhood.

19.   Describe the findings of the Robbers Cave Experiment.

20.   Discuss how social-cognitive abilities, such as social problem-solving skills, may be important to the development of peer relations.

21.   Discuss the role of peers as models and as agents of reinforcement and punishment.

22.   Discuss the relative influences of peers and parents on children's behaviours, attitudes, and choices.

23.   Describe how older and younger children differ in their conceptions of friendship.

24.   Discuss how similarity influences children's selection of friends.

25.   Briefly describe the aspects of interaction that differentiate children who become friends from those who do not, according to John Gottman's research.

26.   Compare and contrast children's behaviour with friends and non-friends, in terms of prosocial behaviours, conflict and its resolution, and intimacy.

27.   Discuss how friendship can be beneficial for children's self-esteem and social support.

28.   Compare three types of sociometric techniques. Do sociometric measures yield a valid picture of a child's social standing?

29.   Describe the indirect and the behavioural correlates of popularity in children.

30.   Contrast *rejected*, *neglected*, and *controversial* children. How do these children differ? Will they outgrow their problems?

31.   Describe several intervention approaches that have been used to help children with problems in peer relations.

32.   Describe the behaviour of shy/withdrawn children. How are such children viewed by peers and teachers?

33.   Discuss several intervention approaches that have been used to help shy/withdrawn children.

34.   Explain how culture may influence the sociometric status of aggressive children and shy/withdrawn children.

35.   Compare and contrast children's sibling relationships with their peer relationships.

36.   Discuss how security of attachment in infancy is related to later peer relationships.

37.   Outline four ways in which parents can serve as managers, influencing the frequency and nature of their children's peer interactions.

38.   Discuss how parental discipline methods are related to children's peer relationships.

39.   Describe four ways in which positive peer relations can serve as protective factors against family adversity.

KEY TERMS

Parental warmth _____

_____

Parental control _____

_____

Parenting style _____

_____

Authoritative parenting _____

_____

Authoritarian parenting _____

_____

Permissive parenting _____

_____

Uninvolved (disengaged) parenting _____

_____

Sibling rivalry _____

_____

Extended family _____

_____

Blended family _____

_____

Pretend play _____

_____

Parallel play _____

_____

Group _____

_____

Clique _____

_____

Crowds _____

_____

Social problem-solving skills _____

_____

Friendship _____

_____

Behavioural homophyly _____

_____

Social support _____

_____

Sociometric techniques _____

_____

Rejected child _____

_____

Neglected child _____

_____

Controversial child   _____

_____

Social withdrawal   _____

_____

Peer-mediated intervention   _____

_____

Resilient children   _____

_____

FILL-IN EXERCISES

Fill in the word or words that best fit in the spaces below.

1.   According to social learning theory, both parents and peers affect a child's behaviour through _____ and _____ behaviour, and through _____ learning that results from exposure to models.

2.   To Piaget, children's relations with adults are characterized by an imbalance of power in which adults are in authority, whereas their relationship with peers is much more one of _____.

3.   Parents who are low in warmth but high in control are referred to as _____, whereas those who are high in both warmth and control are labelled _____. Those who are high in warmth but low in control are referred to as _____, while those who are low in both warmth and control have been called _____.

4.   Children who are impulsive, immature, and disobedient may have been raised by _____ parents.

5.   Competitive feelings between two or more siblings are referred to as _____ _____.

6.   The term _____ family refers to a family unit that consists not only of parents and children, but also of at least one and sometimes several other adult relatives.

7.   The negative consequences of divorce appear greater for _____ *(boys/girls)* than for _____ *(boys/girls)*.

8.   A(n) _____ family refers to a new family unit, resulting from remarriage, that consists of parents and children from previously separate families.

9.   Infants' initial interactions with peers are characterized as _____-centred.

10.   Play that involves using an object or person to symbolize something else is described as _____ play.

11.   A form of play in which children play next to each other and with similar materials, but with no real cooperation, is referred to as _____ play.

12.   The term _____ refers to a collection of children who interact regularly in a consistent, structured fashion and who share values and a sense of belonging. Some adolescents belong to a collection called a _____, consisting of five to 10 members whose shared interests and behaviour patterns set them apart from their peers.

13.   The skills needed to resolve social dilemmas are referred to as social _____-_____ skills.

14.   Research has shown simple forms of peer imitation in toddlers as young as _____ to _____ months.

15.   Although even young children realize the importance of mutual liking between friends, it is only in late childhood or adolescence that qualities such as _____ and _____ become central to children's thinking about friendship.

16.   One general factor central to most friendships is _____. The most important aspect of this factor focuses on behaviours and interests, and is referred to by psychologists as behavioural _____.

17.   Perhaps the most general benefit of friendship is that it provides _____ _____ , that is, resources provided by other people in times of uncertainty or stress.

18.   The sociometric technique in which children are asked "Tell me the names of three kids in the class you especially like" is referred to as the _____ technique.

19.   Three sets of social skills are especially important for popularity; popular children are skilled at _____ interaction with other children, _____ interaction, and at _____ conflict.

20.   A child who receives both many positive and many negative sociometric nominations is referred to as _____.

21.   The most consistent correlate of peer rejection is _____.

22.   Neglected children are often perceived by their peers as being _____. In China, however, children who display such behaviour are more likely to be _____ (below/above) average in popularity.

23. Self-imposed isolation from the peer group is referred to as _____ _____.

24. In addition to training in social skills, rejected children have been helped through training in _____ skills. Such training appears to improve their status in the peer group, perhaps as a result of the subsequent improvement in their self-concept and general classroom behaviour.

25. The home lives of children with peer relations problems may be characterized by parents' use of _____ _____ as a discipline technique.

26. Children who adapt positively and develop well despite early environmental adversity are described as _____ children.

USING WHAT YOU HAVE LEARNED

Having just completed a course in child psychology, you find that your friends are always consulting you concerning issues related to children and families they know. This week is no exception. A friend asks to talk with you about a family she knows that is just going through a divorce. She has questions about the following issues. Based on what you've read, what would you say?

1. Does divorce affect kids?

2. Will the effects "wear off" soon, or are there long-lasting effects on children?

3. What kinds of changes in children's lives after the divorce may be important in terms of how children react?

4. The children will be living with their mom. Is contact with their dad important?

5. If their mom remarries, what issues might they expect in their new, "blended" family? Might there be differences in how the boys react, compared to the girls? What if their dad remarries?

APPLICATION

Situation

Suppose you were to design an intervention program for rejected children. The intent of the program would be to teach the participants skills that would enable them to interact better with their peers, with the goal of improving their acceptance in the peer group.

Questions to answer

1. How would you initially identify the rejected children to participate in the intervention program?

2. Based on what you've read in the chapter, what sorts of skills would be important to teach the children?

3. What sorts of approaches would you employ to teach these skills?

4. How could you determine whether your intervention had been successful? What sort of research design would you use (look back to Chapter 2 to refresh your memory)?

SAMPLE TEST QUESTIONS

1. According to Piaget's theory, interaction with peers is important as it leads to the ability to consider different perspectives, resulting in:

a.	moral realism	b.	moral relativism
c.	moral dilemma	d.	moral comparison

2. Parents who are loving and emotionally sensitive, but set few limits on behaviour and provide little in the way of structure or predictability, are described as:

    a.   authoritarian
    b.   permissive
    c.   uninvolved
    d.   authoritative

3. Deborah developed an insecure attachment to her parents as an infant. As a child, she showed low social competence and did poorly in school. As an adolescent, she has frequently been in trouble with the law and uses drugs a lot. In terms of parenting style, her parents likely:

    a.   set few limits and provide little by way of attention or support
    b.   are very demanding and enforce their demands with threats and punishment
    c.   are caring and sensitive, and maintain a predictable environment
    d.   set few limits, but provide encouragement and support

4.   Studies examining father–infant attachment show that:

a.   infants rarely develop an attachment relationship with their fathers
b.   attachment can be as secure with the father as with the mother
c.   even when father and baby have a very secure relationship, it is probably not at strong as the baby's relationship with the mother
d.   all of the above

5.   Which of the following is true concerning siblings?

a.   Because temperaments are heritable, most siblings have similar temperaments.
b.   Siblings with difficult temperaments tend to get along best if both share this temperament.
c.   Siblings typically get along best when they have similar temperaments.
d.   All of the above

6.   A family unit that consists not only of parents and children, but also of at least one and sometimes several other relatives, is called a(n):

a.   blended family
b.   mixed family
c.   unconventional
d.   extended family

7.   Which of the following is true concerning the effects of divorce?

a.   The effects are most evident in the time period immediately following the divorce.
b.   The effects of divorce generally dissipate with time and completely disappear by adolescence.
c.   Girls are more likely to react to divorce with increased aggression and defiant behaviour.
d.   All of the above

8.   Within seven years of their parents' separation, what percentage of Canadian children have been introduced to one or more new step-parents?

a.   10%
b.   33%
c.   50%
d.   75%

9.   In terms of international adoption rates, the most popular choice for Canadian parents is:

a.   older girls
b.   older boys
c.   younger girls
d.   younger boys

10.   Children younger than grade-school age rarely engage in:

    a.   games with rules
    b.   functional play
    c.   constructive play
    d.   pretend play

11.   Two-year-old Janey loves to bang her building blocks together, over and over again. This type of play is best categorized as

    a.   constructive play
    b.   functional play
    c.   pretend play
    d.   games with rules

12.   In preschool-aged children, imitating peers is generally:

    a.   regarded negatively, as it is viewed as making fun of others
    b.   unlikely to occur, as it requires more advanced cognitive abilities
    c.   responded to positively
    d.   largely ignored by other children

13.   Which of the following is **NOT** true about relationships between friends?

    a.   Conflict occurs less often among friends than among non-friends.
    b.   Children share more with friends than with non-friends.
    c.   Children are more likely to engage in self-disclosure with friends than with non-friends.
    d.   All of the above **ARE** true about relationships with friends.

14.   Which of the following are categories of children's social supports?

    a.   informational support
    b.   instrumental support
    c.   emotional support
    d.   all of the above

15.   Which technique for measuring popularity involves naming some specific number of well-liked peers?

    a.   paired-comparison technique
    b.   rating-scale technique
    c.   nomination technique
    d.   sociogram technique

16.   The principal difference between rejected and neglected children is that:

    a.   although both receive few positive nominations, rejected children also receive few negative nominations

    b.   although both receive few positive nominations, neglected children also receive few negative nominations

    c.   although both receive few negative nominations, rejected children also receive few positive nominations

    d.   although both receive few negative nominations, neglected children also receive few positive nominations

17.   Which of the following describes the behaviour of neglected children?

    a.   disruptive behaviour

    b.   overly intrusive attempts to enter groups

    c.   fewer and more hesitant attempts to enter groups

    d.   antisocial, inappropriate behaviour

18.   Which of the following techniques have been found to be effective interventions with children with peer relationship problems?

    a.   teaching perspective-taking skills

    b.   training in social problem-solving abilities

    c.   training in academic skills

    d.   all of the above

19.   Longitudinal studies indicate that:

    a.   children almost always outgrow their peer relationship problems

    b.   compared to neglect, peer rejection is not very stable over time

    c.   neglected children are at risk for later juvenile delinquency

    d.   rejected children are at risk for problems later in life

20.   Ladd identified four roles parents may play as managers, influencing the frequency and nature of their children's peer interactions. Parents may serve as:

    a.   designers, mediators, supervisors, consultants

    b.   reinforcers, punishers, mediators, supervisors

    c.   discipline agents, mediators, supervisors, consultants

    d.   providers of social support, attachment-figures, caregivers, nurturers

ANSWERS

FILL-IN EXERCISES

1. reinforcing; punishing; observational 2. equals 3. authoritarian; authoritative; permissive; uninvolved (disengaged) 4. permissive 5. sibling rivalry 6. extended 7. boys; girls 8. blended 9. object
10. pretend 11. parallel 12. group; clique 13. problem-solving 14. fifteen; twenty 15. loyalty; intimacy
16. similarity; homophyly 17. social support 18. nomination 19. initiating; maintaining; resolving
20. controversial 21. aggression 22. shy; above 23. social withdrawal 24. academic
25. power assertion 26. resilient

USING WHAT YOU HAVE LEARNED

1. Yes, divorce often affects kids negatively.
2. The effects are most evident in the first year or so immediately following the divorce, and generally dissipate with time.
3. Economic changes following the divorce are important. The mother's parenting practices may change. Remarriage and blending of families may also be important.
4. Yes, contact with dad is important. Children adjust most successfully when their relationship with their father is warm and supportive.
5. Boys adjust more readily to remarriage and the presence of a stepfather than do girls. Although less is known about the effects of dad's remarriage, the presence of a stepmother can also be difficult.

APPLICATION

1. Sociometric techniques, either nominations, ratings, or paired comparisons, would be used.
2. The skills should include how to initiate and maintain interactions, and how to resolve conflict.
3. Approaches would include modelling, shaping, and training in perspective taking and social problem-solving. Peer-mediated interventions would be useful.
4. A short-term longitudinal approach could be used, examining children's sociometric status before and after the intervention.

SAMPLE TEST QUESTIONS

1. b	11. b
2. b	12. c
3. a	13. a
4. b	14. d
5. c	15. c
6. d	16. b
7. a	17. c
8. d	18. d
9. c	19. d
10. a	20. a

Chapter 16
Gender-Role Development and Sex Differences

OUTLINE

Use this outline as you read the chapter. Enter your questions, comments, and notes in the space provided. Write down terms or statements you don't understand, with their page numbers.

THEORIES OF GENDER-ROLE DEVELOPMENT AND SEX DIFFERENCES
Learning Objective 16.1: Understand four theoretical approaches to gender development.

Evolutionary and Biological Approaches

Sociocultural Approaches

Cognitive-Developmental Approaches

Environmental/Learning Approaches

SOME PERCEIVED AND REAL SEX DIFFERENCES
Learning Objective 16.2: Describe physical, cognitive, and social/personality sex differences that have been found.

Physical Differences

Cognitive Differences

Application
Should Schools Teach Visual-Spatial Skills?

Social and Personality Differences

BIOLOGICAL INFLUENCES ON GENDER-ROLE DEVELOPMENT
Learning Objective 16.3: Understand the role of biological influences in the development of sex differences.

Genetic Influences

Hormonal Influences

Brain Lateralization

Research Classic
When Nature and Nurture Conflict

SOCIALIZATION AND GENDER-ROLE DEVELOPMENT
Learning Objective 16.4: Understand how society, parents, peers, and the self contribute to gender-role socialization.

Socialization by Society

Socialization by Parents

Socialization by Peers

Socialization by Self

UNDERSTANDING GENDER ROLES AND STEREOTYPES
Learning Objective 16.5: Trace the development of gender-role knowledge and behaviour.

The Development of Gender Identity

The Development of Gender Knowledge

Focus on Research
Preferential Looking as a Measure of Infants' Awareness of Gender-Stereotyped Activities

Flexibility of Gender Knowledge

Gender Knowledge and Behaviour

DEVELOPMENT OF SEXUAL RELATIONSHIPS AND BEHAVIOUR

Learning Objective 16.6: Discuss the development of sexual relationships and behaviour.

Emergence of Romantic and Sexual Interest

Origins of Sexual Orientation

SHORT-ANSWER QUESTIONS

Upon completion of Chapter 16 you should be able to discuss the following topics. Check off those you are confident that you can discuss well. Re-read the material in the text for the topics about which you are less confident. Record the important points from your reading in the space below each topic.

1.   Describe the evolutionary and psychobiological approaches to sex differences and explain how these approaches differ from sociocultural approaches.

2.   Outline Kohlberg's three stages representing the child's understanding of gender constancy.

3.   Explain the origins and effects of gender schemas.

4.   Compare and contrast gender schema theory with Kohlberg's gender constancy theory.

5.   Explain how social learning theorists account for gender-role development.

6.   Describe the physical differences between males and females in the following areas: physical maturity and vulnerability, activity level, and motor development.

7.   Explain how males and females differ in terms of language and verbal abilities.

8.   Discuss the differences found between boys and girls in mathematical abilities, and explain how strategy preferences may contribute to such differences.

9.   Describe the differences in spatial abilities found between boys and girls, and discuss two possible explanations for such differences.

10.   Describe the aspects of infant temperament found to differ between boys and girls.

11.   Explain the differences between girls and boys in emotional development.

12.   Describe how girls differ from boys in the development of self-control.

13.   Discuss how boys and girls differ in aggression and prosocial behaviour.

14.   Explain how girls and boys differ in activities and interests.

15.   Describe the differences found between girls' and boys' peer relationships.

16.   Explain how genetic and hormonal factors contribute to sex differentiation.

17.   Describe the following two hormonal abnormalities: *congenital adrenal hyperplasia (CAH)* and *androgen insensitivity.*

18.   Discuss the roles of biology and socialization in determining gender identity.

19.   Describe how differences between males and females in brain lateralization may play a role in gender differences.

20.   Explain the roles played by society in the socialization of gender roles. What has research shown about the role teachers may play?

21.   Explain the roles played by parents in the socialization of gender roles, commenting on differences in how mothers and fathers socialize their sons and daughters.

22.   Discuss the roles of peers in the socialization of gender roles.

23.   Explain how children participate in their own socialization of gender roles.

24.   Describe how children's gender knowledge and the flexibility of their gender stereotypes develop across age.

25.   Discuss how *preferential looking* has been used to assess infants' awareness of gender-stereotyped activities.

26.   Explain how children's gender knowledge affects their behaviour in the areas of toy preferences, motivation, memory, and social judgments.

27.   Describe the development of romantic and sexual interest.

28.   Discuss how biology and socialization may influence sexual orientation, and describe the interactionist model proposed by Darryl Bem.

KEY TERMS

Upon completion of Chapter 16, you should be able to define the following terms.

Sex differentiation   _____

_____

Gender role   _____

_____

Sex typing   _____

_____

Gender constancy   _____

_____

Gender identity _____

_____

Gender stability _____

_____

Gender consistency   _____

_____

Gender schemas   _____

_____

Meta-analysis   _____

_____

Lateralization   _____

_____

Sex-limited traits   _____

_____

Congenital adrenal hyperplasia (CAH)   _____

_____

Androgen insensitivity   _____

_____

FILL-IN EXERCISES

Fill in the word or words that best fit in the spaces below.

1.   The term _____ _____ refers to a pattern or set of behaviours considered appropriate for males and females within a particular culture.

2.   According to evolutionary approaches, _____ *(males/females)* tend to be choosier about their mates and invest more in parenting.

3.   According to the _____ approach, gender roles develop as children participate in and prepare for the adult roles they are expected to play in their communities.

4.   Kohlberg proposed that gender constancy develops in the following three stages: gender _____, gender _____, and gender _____.

5.   Gender _____ are cognitive representations of the characteristics associated with being either male or female.

6.   At birth, the _____ *(male/female)* newborn is generally healthier and more developmentally advanced.

7.   On average, _____ *(boys/girls)* have higher activity levels, a difference that extends through infancy and childhood.

8.   _____ *(boys/girls)* show an advantage in motor skills that require a combination of balance and precise movement.

9.   Throughout the school years _____ *(boys/girls)* achieve higher scores in reading and writing.

10.   Brain _____ refers to the specialization of functions in the right and left hemispheres of the brain.

11.   Starting in first-grade, girls are more likely to use _____ mathematical strategies, whereas boys are more likely to use _____ approaches.

12.   There is some evidence that sex differences in spatial abilities _____ *(increase/decrease)* in adolescence and adulthood.

13.   _____ *(male/female)* infants seem better equipped for socialization. They maintain greater eye contact, engage in more face-to-face communication, and smile more.

14.   Sex differences have been reported in strategies used to regulate emotional states. Toddlers were promised an attractive toy but made to wait before being allowed to play with it. The _____ (*boys/girls*) coped with the stress of the situation by seeking comfort from their mothers, whereas the _____ (*boys/girls*) were more likely to distract themselves by playing with other objects in the room.

15.   Boys are _____ (*more/less*) likely to express anger, _____ (*more/less*) likely to deny feeling afraid, and _____ (*more/less*) likely to follow cultural display rules regarding the expression of disappointment.

16.   Prior to age _____, girls and boys engage in disruptive and impulsive behaviour equally often. After this age, however, _____ (*boys/girls*) show a steady decline in behaviour problems, whereas _____ (*boys/girls*) show a lesser decline and, in some cases, even an increase.

17.   In elementary school, girls show _____ interest in mathematics and science compared to boys.

18.   Specific interests within the domain of science differ between boys and girls. Male students tend to express more interest in the _____ sciences, whereas female students express more interest in the _____ sciences.

19.   Beginning in early childhood, _____ (*boys/girls*) play in larger groups, whereas _____ (*boys/girls*) generally limit their group size to two or three.

20.   Like most other species, humans exhibit sexual _____ —that is, the male and female are biologically different for the purpose of reproduction. The process through which these biological differences emerge is called sex _____.

21.   Traits resulting from genes that affect males and females differently but that are not carried on the sex chromosomes are referred to as sex _____ traits.

22.   When a Y chromosome causes testes to develop in the embryo, these glands secrete hormones called _____, which cause the male internal organs to grow.

23.   Congenital _____ _____ is a recessive genetic disorder in which the adrenal glands produce unusually high levels of male hormones, regardless of the presence or absence of testes.

24.   Studies show consistently that teachers give more attention to _____ (*boys/girls*) than to _____(*boys/girls*).

25.   During infancy, parents are more likely to physically stimulate _____ (*boys/girls*) than _____ (*boys/girls*).

26.   Parents' gender typing of play tends to be stronger with _____ (*sons/daughters*) than with _____ (*sons/daughters*). This is especially true of _____ (*mothers/fathers*).

27. Data from a number of studies have confirmed Kohlberg's stage model of gender constancy. By 3 years of age, almost all children display gender _____. Gender _____ follows at about 4 years of age, and gender _____ at about 5.

28. Gender knowledge has been found to influence children's memory. Children's recall is better when it is _____ with the gender schemas they have formed.

29. Surveys in North America and Europe estimated the percentage of men who identify themselves as gay to be around _____ to _____ of the population, and the percentage of women who identify themselves as lesbian to be around _____ to _____. The proportions are higher if the criteria include same-sex _____ _____ without self-identification as gay or lesbian.

30. Bem has proposed a model—termed the _____-_____-_____ theory—of how biological factors and experience might interact in the development of sexual orientation.

APPLICATION

You have read in Chapter 16 about differences between boys and girls in certain cognitive abilities and certain social and personality characteristics. Some of these may have a biological basis; some may be the result of differences in how adults socialize children; most of them probably involve an interaction between nature and nurture. Using what you have read in Chapter 16, consider how nature and nurture may play a role in the following sex differences, and especially consider how they may interact.

1. On average, girls have greater abilities in many types of verbal skills than boys.

2. By adolescence, males express greater interest in mathematics than do females. They also begin to perform significantly better than females, at least when measured on standardized exams.

3. On average, boys seem to be better at spatial tasks such as mental-rotation tasks, a sex difference that may increase during adolescence.

4. On average, boys have higher activity levels than girls. Interestingly, sex differences in activity level are small when children are playing alone; however, boys' activity levels increase substantially when they are in the company of other boys.

5. Boys generally display more aggressive behaviour than girls.

USING WHAT YOU HAVE LEARNED

What are Some Common Beliefs About Sex Differences?

Many people hold stereotypical beliefs about sex differences. It can be interesting to compare these with what research actually shows about how males and females differ. To get an idea of some of these beliefs, ask several of your friends how boys and girls differ and what they think is the source of these differences.

1.   What seem to be the most common beliefs?

2.   Is there an age difference in beliefs? That is, do older people have different beliefs than younger people?

3.   Is there a gender difference in beliefs? That is, do males hold different beliefs or offer different explanations for the source of gender differences than females?

4.   Does providing objective information about gender differences alter people's beliefs? Think about your own beliefs before and after reading Chapter 16. Did they change?

SAMPLE TEST QUESTIONS

1.   The process by which biological sex differences emerge is referred to as:

     a.   sex typing
     b.   gender typing
     c.   gender identity formation
     d.   sex differentiation

2.   According to Kohlberg's theory, children pass through three stages in the development of gender constancy. The order of these stages is:

     a.   gender identity, gender stability, gender consistency
     b.   gender consistency, gender identity, gender stability
     c.   gender identity, gender consistency, gender stability
     d.   gender stability, gender identity, gender consistency

3.   Sociocultural theorists contend that

     a.   sex differences observed among children and adults follow from the roles commonly held by females versus males
     b.   inborn, intrinsic differences between the sexes give rise to and maintain gender roles
     c.   the cognitive representations children have of the characteristics associated with being either male or female underlie children's gender-role behaviour
     d.   sex-typed behaviours are the product of reinforcement and modelling

4.   All of the following are ways in which female newborns differ from male newborns, **EXCEPT:**

    a.   the female is healthier and more developmentally advanced than the male
    b.   the female is less muscular than the male
    c.   the female is less sensitive to pain than the male
    d.   the female is better coordinated neurologically and physically

5.   By about age 5, boys perform better than girls on tasks requiring

    a.   balance and precise movement
    b.   fine motor skills
    c.   strength
    d.   all of the above

6.   Which of the following is untrue concerning language and verbal abilities in female infants?

    a.   Female infants produce fewer sounds than do males.
    b.   Female infants use words earlier than males.
    c.   Female infants have a larger vocabulary than males.
    d.   All of the above **ARE** true.

7.   Which of the following is true concerning the mathematical strategies preferred by girls?

    a.   Girls prefer to use logic, estimation, and unconventional strategies to solve mathematical problems.
    b.   Girls prefer the conventional strategies that are taught in school.
    c.   Starting in the first grade, girls prefer to use more sophisticated strategies than do boys.
    d.   All of the above

8.   Ross Vasta and colleagues' finding that bartenders and servers perform better than adults of equal age, gender, and education on the water-level task suggests that

    a.   performance on the water-level task is culturally specific
    b.   practical experience can enhance spatial competence
    c.   spatial competence is largely biologically based
    d.   spatial competence is evolutionarily based

9.   Which of the following is untrue concerning the social interactions of female infants?

    a.   Female infants maintain greater eye contact with their caregivers than males.
    b.   Female infants engage in more face-to-face communication than males.
    c.   Female infants smile more during social interactions than do males.
    d.   Female infants are more sociable than males.

10.   In terms of the development of self-control,

   a.   boys develop self-regulatory capabilities more rapidly than girls
   b.   boys comply more readily and at a younger age than girls
   c.   boys engage in more disruptive and impulsive behaviour than girls, even as toddlers
   d.   none of the above

11.   Which of the following is untrue concerning aggression and prosocial behaviour in girls and boys?

   a.   Boys display more physical aggression than girls.
   b.   Girls are more likely to display relational and social forms of aggression than boys.
   c.   Girls tend to display more prosocial behaviour than boys.
   d.   Actually, all of the above **ARE** true.

12.   The sex chromosomes

   a.   influence the prenatal development of the male gonads at about six weeks
   b.   influence the prenatal development of the female gonads at about six weeks
   c.   play a crucial role in sex differentiation throughout the prenatal period
   d.   all of the above

13.   Congenital adrenal hyperplasia results in:

   a.   higher levels of aggressive and antisocial behaviour in boys
   b.   masculinized interests and activities in girls
   c.   feminized interests and activities in boys
   d.   markedly high spatial abilities in boys

14.   How do teachers often react when children engage in cross-sex activities?

   a.   Both boys and girls receive criticism equally for engaging in cross-sex activities.
   b.   Both boys and girls are encouraged to engage in cross-sex activities.
   c.   Girls receive criticism for engaging in cross-sex activities more than do boys.
   d.   Boys receive criticism for engaging in cross-sex activities more than do girls.

15.   When do parents begin to view boys and girls differently?

   a.   at birth
   b.   shortly after the first birthday
   c.   during the toddler period
   d.   during the preschool period

16.   How do fathers differ from mothers in the role they play in gender-role development?

   a.   Mothers play the largest role; fathers, because they spend less time with their children, contribute very little.
   b.   Mothers are concerned that their daughters be feminine; fathers are concerned that their sons be masculine.
   c.   Fathers are concerned that their daughters be feminine and their sons be masculine, whereas mothers are less concerned about the gender-appropriateness of their children's behaviour.
   d.   Mothers are concerned that their daughters be feminine and their sons be masculine, whereas fathers are less concerned about the gender-appropriateness of their children's behaviour.

17.   Children can reliably sort pictures of males and females and their "accessories" such as toys, tools, and appliances by about what age?

   a.   one year
   b.   two years
   c.   three years
   d.   four years

18.   After being shown a series of photographs depicting either a male or a female performing a sex-stereotyped activity (e.g., a woman or a man ironing clothes), children were asked which pictures they had seen. Children:

   a.   more accurately remembered gender-inconsistent information than consistent information, probably because it seemed so different to them that it stuck in their minds
   c.   remembered both gender consistent and inconsistent information equally well
   d.   could not remember either gender consistent or inconsistent information, since visual memory is so poor in children
   d.   more accurately remembered gender-consistent than inconsistent information

19.   Boys and girls typically report experiencing their first romantic interests, or "crushes"

   a.   between the ages of 5 and 7
   b.   between the ages of 7 and 10
   c.   between the ages of 10 and 14
   d.   between the ages of 15 and 16

20.   Which of the following is true concerning homosexual men?

   a.   Homosexual men tend frequently to be first-borns.
   b.   Homosexual men tend be the only boy in a family with many older sisters.
   c.   Homosexual men are more likely to have several older brothers than heterosexual men.
   d.   Homosexual men tend frequently to have a father who is gay.

ANSWERS

FILL-IN EXERCISES

1. gender role   2. females   3. sociocultural   4. identity, stability, consistency   5. schemas
6. female   7. boys   8. girls   9. girls   10. lateralization   11. concrete; abstract   12. increase
13. female   14. girls; boys   15. more; more; less   16. 4 or 5 years; girls; boys   17. equal
18. physical; people-oriented (or biological and health)   19. boys; girls   20. dimorphism; differentiation   21. limited   22. androgens   23. adrenal hyperplasia (CAH)   24. boys; girls   25. boys; girls
26. sons; daughters; fathers   27. identity; stability; four; consistency   28. consistent   29. 3%; 5%; 2%; 3%; romantic attraction   30. Exotic-Becomes-Erotic

APPLICATION

1. Female superiority on verbal and language tasks may derive from the fact that they use both hemispheres to process language, in contrast with males whose language abilities are localized in the left hemisphere. However, girls also usually experience a richer language environment than boys.

2. Brain lateralization and differences in spatial abilities may account to some extent for differences in mathematics abilities. However, strategy differences between the sexes and differences in comfort with the possibility of making mistakes may also explain the differing performance of boys and girls. Socialization is also important.

3. Brain lateralization is important; however, from early childhood on, boys also spend more time in activities that promote spatial skills than do girls.

4. There may be hormonal effects influencing activity level; however, modelling, as well as differential treatment of boys and girls by parents and teachers, likely also play a role.

5. Hormonal differences likely play an important role in aggression. Modelling, differential treatment of boys and girls by parents and teachers, and different societal expectations are also likely quite important.

SAMPLE TEST QUESTIONS

1. d	11. c
2. a	12. a
3. a	13. b
4. c	14. d
5. c	15. a
6. a	16. c
7. b	17. b
8. b	18. d
9. d	19. b
10. d	20. c

NOTES

NOTES

NOTES

NOTES

NOTES

NOTES